MAKE YOUR
FAMILY
RICH

MAKE YOUR FAMILY RICH

Why to Replace Retirement Planning with Succession Planning

PATRICK J. KEOGH

Stonebrook Publishing
Saint Louis, Missouri

STONEBROOK
PUBLISHING

STONEBROOK
PUBLISHING

A STONEBROOK PUBLISHING BOOK
©2020 Patrick J. Keogh

Library of Congress Control Number: 2020904738

ISBN: 978-1-7339958-9-4

www.stonebrookpublishing.net

PRINTED IN THE UNITED STATES OF AMERICA

10   9   8   7   6   5   4   3   2   1

DEDICATION

To Annie and John Keogh (Mom and Pop),
the best investors ever

CONTENTS

Introduction	9
1: The Business Cycle	17
2: Getting Started—Generating Your Seed Money	23
3: The Goal—Make Your Family Rich	29
4: Go Long on America and Only America	37
5: How to Avoid the Gnu Effect	53
6: When, How, and How Much to Buy	71
7: DRIP, DRIP, DRIP—Compound Interest on Steroids	95
8: When and How to Sell	99
9: Scratch That Itch	101
10: Not All Debt Is Bad All the Time	105
11: Remember, It's All Negotiable	111
12: Investing in Real Estate	115
13: Beyond Estate Planning: Succession Planning	155
14: Move to the Rich Neighborhood	167
15: The Guiding Principles at a Glance	179
Epilogue	181
Acknowledgments	185
About the Author	187

INTRODUCTION

THIS BOOK STEMS FROM THE ONGOING NATIONAL discussion about the decline of the middle class and the rising number of people living in poverty. Nearly every day, we hear more data about the loss of "good paying jobs" and the "broken social compact." Americans once thought that if they got an education and worked hard, they'd achieve a middle-class lifestyle. Some folks think that's not true anymore. President Obama never seemed to miss an opportunity to commiserate with the declining middle class and beat the drum about shifting wealth from the "fortunate" few to that shrinking middle class demographic.

Politically speaking, the rhetoric has only gotten worse. Several candidates vying for the 2020 presidential nomination agree that the role of government is to cure poverty. One candidate frequently says there's plenty of money around; it's just in the wrong hands—implying he intends to put it in the right hands.

Whatever happened to the "shining city on a hill" that Ronald Reagan envisioned? It now seems to be a gated community that only the fortunate few can enter. Where's the inspirational leadership?

The real problem is that people who think the opportunity to get rich is dead or diminished have a depressing effect not only on themselves, but, more importantly, on the rest of us. People tend to absorb repetitive messaging, particularly when it comes from authority figures.

I hear others using the same language supported by misleading statistics. I regularly receive emails from my friends singing the dirge of the declining middle class, income inequality, and growing poverty. A local attorney I work with takes every opportunity to tell me I've buried my head in the sand when I fail to acknowledge this serious national problem.

I don't see poverty as a handicap. I view it as a starting point. In this country, there's no reason to stay poor. You can't help being born into poverty, but you don't have to stay there. In fact, I believe that coming into this world poor, particularly in the US, can be an advantage because the poor person has an incentive to work harder and save. In my view, if you weren't born with a silver spoon in your mouth, count your blessings.

However, it's difficult to find a political leader who believes that. It's become many politicians' stock-in-trade to define "poor" as just another disability. They offer programs to solve the problem of poverty in exchange for votes.

Other political leaders see poverty as simply the absence of wealth. Who has all that wealth? Well, it's the rich, they say. These politicians believe we have a maldistribution of wealth in this country, and they think it's their job to use government to transfer that wealth. They propose taxing financial success to provide for those less fortunate. That approach could take the form of a wealth tax, a high estate tax, or simply higher capital gains or additional income tax on high earners.

They'd redistribute that wealth to the poor in a variety of forms, such as a guaranteed annual income, guaranteed government jobs, free college tuition, free healthcare, or a range of other entitlements. It seems this attitude comes from a view that there's only so much wealth. If our society's wealth were a pie, that pie would be a fixed size. I don't see it that way. We can each bake bigger pies for ourselves and our families, and that's what this book is about.

> *We can each bake bigger pies for ourselves and our families, and that's what this book is about.*

Throughout the world, many people seem to resent others' financial success. I've heard it called the tall poppy syndrome. If any poppy in the field grows substantially higher than the other poppies, then it's government's job to cut that poppy down to the size of the others. I think that's a destructive way to see the world and wealth creation.

While some people throw a national wet blanket on initiative, the media sometimes features young people who've grown new-found businesses to billion-dollar enterprises in a few short years. These entrepreneurs invested their own limited capital to create new products and generate enormous wealth for themselves and society. That's one way to get rich in America today, and nowhere on Earth are the startup paths to entrepreneurial wealth better than in the US. However, that's a bit like focusing on your basketball game and hoping to make the NBA.

This book isn't about how to take a great idea and create a billion-dollar business, but I believe the people doing that have followed many of the principles I lay out here. Nor is this book about learning to live in an economically diminished America, though living in moderation is a key principle we embrace.

Certain educational opportunities and professions can help you achieve wealth. If you become a brain surgeon or a corporate lawyer, you'll probably attain a comfortable lifestyle. If you have those skills and ambitions, then go for it. This book will help you capitalize on the income you generate from your profession.

At its core, this book demonstrates how to get rich by planning and working to make your family rich. Read that sentence again. That's an essential point I develop. The best way for you to get rich is to focus on making your family rich. You'll achieve sustained family wealth as you accumulate capital and train your successors in the principles and systems outlined in this book. You can do that while you pursue your career and eventually migrate into the business of managing the capital you accumulated and educating your heirs on how to continue to manage and grow their capital. In modern America, it's the accumulation of capital and the skills necessary to manage capital that create significant and sustainable wealth. Even if you get as rich as an NBA star or a brain surgeon, you won't be able to sustain that wealth for your family unless you adopt the principles and systems in this book.

> *I define rich as being able to buy anything*
> *you need or want for yourself and your family.*

I define *rich* as being able to buy anything you need or want for yourself and your family. *Rich* means you have the freedom to live where you want and travel when and where you desire. It's the ability to provide the best educational opportunities for your family and to give them whatever they need for their health, safety, and welfare. In the end, rich is about freedom. As Mae West put it, "I've been rich, and I've been poor. Rich is better." That's been my experience too.

One caveat. "It takes a village to raise a child" is a popular adage. That village, it seems to me, demonstrates an unconditional love approach to life, meaning if a child gets love and support from the broader community, he or she will be a happier, better adjusted person. That's probably true as far as it goes, but children must also be trained to function, produce, and prosper. That usually means teaching them delayed gratification, doing things they may not want to do at the moment in order to achieve a goal in the future. Think of the US military. They train some of the world's most productive and virtuous people, but there's not a lot of unconditional love in their training manuals.

It helps to think of delayed gratification in a different way. You may put off some gratification by not committing capital to some consumable or other. If you do that with a larger plan in mind—like making your family rich—then isn't it more like redirected gratification? You and your family get the gratification of seeing the family's wealth and security accumulate. Perhaps you postpone buying that new boat to accelerate the accumulation of capital. After your family is rich and successfully managing the family's asset management business, that's a better time to invest in the boat. Naming the boat *Redirected Gratification* might turn some heads and stimulate conversation at the yacht club. More likely, when you can afford that yacht, you'll have better things to do with the capital and your time.

Parts of this book may offend some readers. I think of it as the tough love version of "it takes a village." It doesn't hurt to live in a nurturing village. But most of all, it takes a parent to show the way and install the right systems and a family succession plan to sustain those systems. We'll suggest you move to a new virtual neighborhood—one where the people around you read the right things and talk and work with others, all striving to be rich. That's where you need to live. Please note, I said virtual neighborhood. You can move there at no cost other than your own effort.

I belong to the American Association of Individual Investors (AAII). It's a group of individuals who come together periodically to discuss various investment opportunities. AAII has a number of local chapters around the country, a periodic newsletter, and an annual convention. Each monthly meeting typically includes a presentation by a professional financial advisor. Technically, they're not there to sell anything, but it's clear their firm or financial products are available should you wish to use their services. Many presentations follow a discussion led by one of the local members, called a SIG, or Special Interest Group. When the head of our SIG asked for volunteers, I offered to give a pitch about my family's approach to investing. I was pleasantly surprised by the positive feedback from the chapter members. Some members are seniors like myself, and I sensed I'd given voice to much of their own experience and provided some answers to how they could best move forward with their investments and families. That led me to expand the presentation, and this book is the product of that effort.

This is a long-term approach to investing. Make no mistake, it's about investing, not trading, although that's a necessary component of investing. I will explain the elements of the system. I'll also detail some personal habits to avoid. At the end, you'll find a summary of my common sense guiding principles. Implementing the system may seem complex at first, but as with most new undertakings, you'll start off slowly but then pick up the pace as it makes more sense.

The number of investing systems and philosophies is unlimited. Many require constant attention and ongoing analysis. Some require the investor to time the buying and selling of individual industries' stocks. Others require periodic rebalancing among various asset classes. It's no wonder would-be investors see investing as too complex and time consuming to fit into their busy lives. That often leads prospective investors to believe they need a financial expert and advisor to sort through all that complexity. I don't think so. That financial advisor or manager is an avoidable expense, and I think you can do better yourself. Typical financial advisors usually earn one percent or more of the value of the assets they manage. One percent may not seem very high, but it adds up, and, over time, it will eat into your returns and the value of your assets.

We think you can manage your own assets without an outside manager if you use the principles and systems in this book. You won't feel that way at first. We advise you to take it slowly. Live the system and adopt the practices we recommend. As you incorporate them into your life, the values and practices we promote will become a comfortable part of your regular routine.

Professional financial advisors will never support the investment approach in this book, even though some of them may believe in it. Why? Because their lawyers won't allow them to do so. We'll explain why in chapter 3.

You are who you hang out with and what you do. You are what you read and watch on TV, and you are how you look and how you speak. You know all that. Sometimes you need a particular incentive to make changes, and the long-term goal of making your family rich and teaching your children how to continue that legacy should be enough motivation.

Our system is based on easily understood and applied common sense and on free data that's readily available. Applying the system will become a daily habit and will require some work. We believe you can easily integrate it into your daily life. As you age, we hope managing your assets will become your life's work. Together with your family, you'll manage the assets you've accumulated over your lifetime. As you learn to understand, manage, grow, and live your assets, you'll enjoy the experience of making your family rich. Perhaps more importantly, you'll take particular satisfaction in implementing your family's succession plan.

In generations past, the farmer and the small business owner took great pride in passing down their skills, their businesses, and their assets to their sons and daughters. At this time and in this country, where the opportunities to accumulate capital and own multiple businesses are so great, we can employ similar systems for our heirs to continue to accumulate capital and sustain the asset management businesses we create. To do that, we need to think and act differently. I hope this book provides the blueprint for the thoughts and actions that will make your family rich!

1

THE BUSINESS CYCLE

OST FOLKS HAVE HEARD OF THE LEGENDARY investor Warren Buffett, the so-called "Oracle of Omaha." He's thought to be among the greatest investors of all time. He's a Will Rogers sort of fellow who seems to reduce complex concepts to home-spun common sense. He's also one of the richest people in the world. In a world that expects an answer for every question and an explanation for every market change, Buffett seems to see things through a different lens. Perhaps what impresses me most about Buffett is his reluctance to give easy answers. In the midst of market turmoil, people have asked him, "Where will the market go tomorrow?" or, "Where will the market be at year end or a year from now?" He always answers, "I don't know." And he follows that with, "But I think I do know where it will be in ten or twenty years." Warren Buffett is an old guy who's invested throughout his adult life. He's seen it all, or almost all. Most significantly, he's continued to accumulate wealth over time through up markets and down markets.

When Buffett says he knows where markets will be at some distant time, he's saying that throughout his very long investing life, the American economy has been down and up, but over time it tends to go up. Several times during his life he saw the market decline by 40 percent or more, and he viewed those times as buying opportunities because he knew the market always comes back. Buffett recognizes the persistence of the American economy's recurring business cycles. I'm not quite as old as Buffett, but I've seen these cycles too.

The business cycle is an economic phenomenon that describes the tendency of the economy to go through a pattern of periods of expansion—where jobs increase, consumer spending and asset values increase, and there's a general sense of prosperity—and periods of economic contraction or decline, often resulting in a recession. Over time, the business cycle looks like a recurring sine wave, as the following chart depicts. In this oversimplified chart, you can see the message Buffett tries to convey. The contractions rarely go down below the level of the prior decline, and when the expansion comes, markets go higher than the previous expansion. Commit this image to memory. The truth of that graph is essential to grasping the investment principles and approach in this book.

THE BUSINESS CYCLE

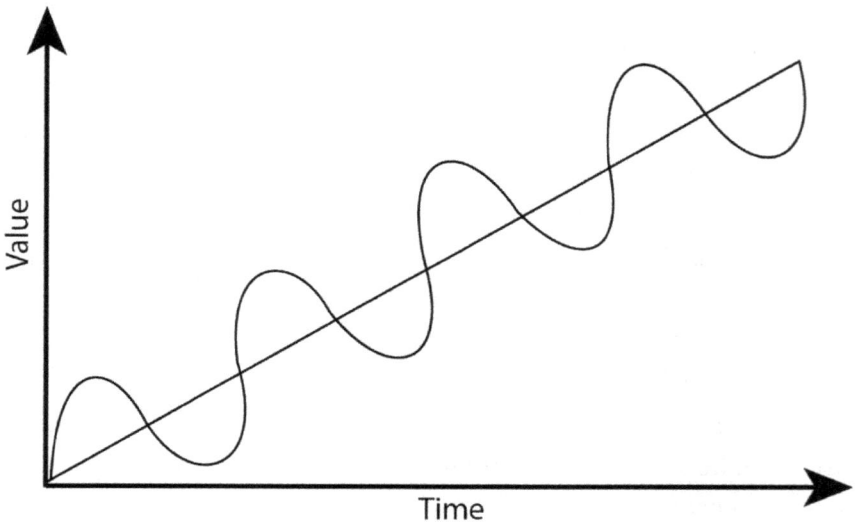

Most asset classes go up during an expansion and come down during a contraction. For example, both the stock market and real estate values go up in an expansion and come down in a contraction. Not necessarily by the same amounts and not in all geographic areas but, as a rule of thumb, assets go up and come down together. So, the best investment strategy is to sell at the peak and buy at the trough, right? No one consistently does that well. Every so often, someone gets it right at least once and then writes a book about his or her 20/20 vision, but most people do just the opposite. That is, they feel good as markets go up and continue to buy and then panic and sell when the market tanks. By doing that, the investor misses the inevitable recovery.

> *The investing system put forth in this book should dissuade you from trying to time the market.*

The investing system put forth in this book should dissuade you from trying to time the market. That's because your investments will mostly or entirely be limited to stocks in businesses that have paid increasing dividends for at least twenty-five years. Stop and think about that. Savor the idea. You'll be buying businesses that paid their owners increasing returns through the likes of the Great Recession and the Tech Bubble. With a long-term or forever horizon, and if you accept the business cycle, there's no bad time to buy those increasing dividend stocks. Even when the market goes down, you'll get regular raises in income, and thereby reduce your tendency to sell in a down market. That will see you through the downdrafts and sustain you to the inevitable higher peaks. Remember, you're not investing for yourself or your retirement. You're investing into perpetuity for your family, so a short-term perspective is almost irrelevant to your investment strategy.

Ignoring down markets is much easier said than done. But with time, your experience will grow, the markets will come back better and higher than before, and you'll receive raises in your income even through down markets. Keep picturing that business cycle graph.

When you focus on your regularly increasing income, it gives you a different perspective to measure your investment performance. Regardless of where market values go, your income will always increase. This perspective and investment approach also gives you more control over your life. You can't control when or whether markets go up or go down. This book and the systems recommended will give you control of your ever-increasing income. In time, we hope you'll come to measure success less by the market value of the businesses you own and more by the ever-increasing income they generate for you and your family.

The positive sloping line in the graph shows two things. First, it illustrates the long-term pattern of increasing asset values over time. In an April 2019 *Barron's* article, "Safe But Not Entirely Sound," Jack Hough wrote, "If stock returns were linear rather than squiggly, every day would bring fresh highs." There's a thought to reflect on when those downdrafts happen. Perhaps Hough's statement makes this very important point even better than the graph. Regardless of any downward squiggle in values, over the long term, values are persistently higher, or unsquiggly.

Buffett's long-time partner, Charlie Munger, may have said it best: "The big money is not in the buying and selling but in the waiting." Savor that. I love that quote.

Now, consider that ascending straight line on the chart. That line defines growing income and the long-term growth in the value of the equities market. Viewed over a long enough time frame, it confirms that US equities are in a perpetual bull market, as Jack Hough suggests. That's why it's imperative to adopt the Make Your Family Rich objective. With that goal, your time frame is forever.

That same graph also shows the gradually increasing income generated from investing in stocks with constantly increasing dividends. Market declines are inevitable. It helps to see that increasing dividend income as the one very healthy dose of sugar that makes palatable the medicine of market declines.

2

GETTING STARTED—GENERATING YOUR SEED MONEY

WHEN DISCUSSING INVESTMENT STRATEGY, I often hear, "How much do I need to get started?" I usually say that the most critical thing is to start saving. Then I hear a resigned response like, "After I pay my bills, I have nothing left over." It's almost as though bills are a constant; they have a life of their own. But we create those bills, and we can reduce or eliminate them. If you need an excuse not to make your family rich, the "after I get my bills paid" one is as good as it gets. That makes you a victim of the bills you created but does nothing to make you or your family rich.

The "after I get my bills paid" response shouldn't surprise anyone. It's hard to listen to business news or read financial journals without learning that "70 percent of the American economy is the consumer." It's not much of a stretch to believe that consumption drives our economy. And if that's true, then consumption is a desirable standard of conduct. Heck, it might even be a patriotic duty.

You may remember that President George W. Bush advised Americans after 9-11 to get out there and go shopping. Shopping almost seemed to be the primary indicator of normal. All you have to do is look in the average garage or check kitchen cabinets and closets to see that Americans have lots of stuff. Check out the big box stores. They're all about selling large volumes of stuff that you take home and store. Isn't that the Costco business plan: from their store to your store? If consuming is patriotic, then we're one very patriotic country.

There's also the constant poverty mantra from government. You know, the "40 percent of Americans can't afford a four-hundred-dollar car repair." It almost seems as if they want you to believe it's okay to be broke because so many others are broke, too, and the government's stock-in-trade is to fix it for you. They have a program for that! It's nonsense.

When was the last time you heard Benjamin Franklin's old adage, "A penny saved is a penny earned"? When you understand the strategy discussed in this book and catch the burning desire to make your family rich, you'll be anxious to accumulate the capital to start that process. It will be good to train yourself to get more joy from saving and watching your capital grow than from consuming. It's okay to accumulate stuff. Just make sure you and your family own shares in great companies. Those are your businesses. (Takes less storage space too!)

> *It will be good to train yourself to get more joy from saving and watching your capital grow than from consuming.*

Start thinking and acting like your savings is the primary amount you commit to set aside, and whatever's left is available to pay your bills. You'll only incur expenses up to the amount of money available after you've contributed to your savings. If you have trouble regularly saving the money you earn from your job, get a second job or start selling stuff you don't use. Do you really need that power washer? Maybe you can delay that Caribbean cruise. What's the big deal about eating out? Who really needs bottled water?

But if you're stuck in the cycle that "after I pay my bills, there's nothing left over," and you insist on sticking by that, then stop reading now. God and this book can only help those who help themselves.

Open a Brokerage Account

As you save, don't put the money in a savings account. Put your savings into a brokerage account, because investing in American businesses will be the principal vehicle you'll use to make your family rich. Everyone in your new neighborhood has a brokerage account, and you need one too. That's right, you've moved to a new virtual neighborhood. More about that later in chapter 14.

Don't worry about how much money you start with. Everyone started at some time with very little. Little is good. That's your incentive to grow. The less you start with, the better you'll do. President Trump makes a big deal about his wealth. According to different stories, he started with either one million dollars from his dad, Fred, or a whole lot more. But he started with something. So, in computing the rate of return over his life, he has a denominator. He's a denominator guy. No matter how much he started with, you can calculate his lifetime rate of return by dividing his current wealth by that initial capital.

Think of your comparative advantage if you start with nothing. You're a zero-denominator guy or gal! Whatever you have in the future is divided by zero dollars. That means you can achieve an infinite rate of return! Infinite is good—very, very good. In fact, you can't beat infinite. So, if you apply the systems in this book, you'll get a better comparative result than Donald Trump. You feel better already, right?

Think about the presidential candidates and ask yourself which candidate has the best opportunity to win. Is it the person who was born poor and made his way up the ladder to that podium, or is it the one who inherited a bundle from his family? Starting poor may be an advantage to a politician. If you're poor, think of it as an advantage. In this country poor is not a handicap; it's simply a starting point.

The Door to the Library Is the Door to Wealth

Barron's is a weekly financial paper that comes out every Saturday and is available online and in print. It's also available in many libraries. It's good to get into the habit of reading *Barron's* every week. If your library doesn't have it, ask them to order a subscription. It never hurts to ask, and why incur the expense if the library will make the publication available to you? *Barron's* periodically reviews the best brokerage firms based on fees and services. I've worked with TD Ameritrade and its predecessor firm, and they typically receive high ratings by *Barron's* for services and have relatively low transaction fees and margin rates.

While you're at the library, get used to reading the *Wall Street Journal*. The *Journal* is published every day except Sunday. It's a great newspaper, available online and in print. Almost every library gets the *Journal*, and if you don't have a second job, the library is a great place to spend time. While you're at the library, also introduce yourself to *Value Line*. It's in the black three-ring binders you see those old rich folks reading. Some libraries have *Value Line* in the print version. Many have it online, available to library members. You can buy subscriptions to all three publications, but why incur the expense when they're all free at the public library? *Value Line* is a particularly important reference material.

Someone once said that education starts at the library door. Maybe getting rich does too.

Someone once said that education starts at the library door. Maybe getting rich does too. They have all the good stuff at the library, or they can get it for you. There's a reason libraries tend to be the only government agencies with citizen fan clubs. Think about that. Doesn't your library have a Friends of the Library organization? Many do. You should join.

You are what you read. Reading *Barron's*, the *Journal*, and *Value Line* will be a bit alien at first. But like learning a new language, you'll gradually come to understand the vocabulary and concepts. These publications contain the stories of many businesses that are familiar to you. Some of them are also the businesses you'll own that will make your family rich. To get rich, it helps to read the material rich people read, and they read publications like *Barron's*, the *Wall Street Journal,* and *Value Line*. Don't fight it. Just start reading them. Your neighbors in the rich neighborhood read these publications. When in Rome . . .

There are a couple of apps that will help you get started too. The first is *Yahoo* and their financial software. Later, we'll discuss how to use *Yahoo* to target opportunities. *Yahoo* will make it much easier to implement the systems and processes recommended in this book.

Seeking Alpha is also very helpful software. It's a crowd-sourced service where investors and professional advisors evaluate various stocks. "Alpha" is simply the financial term for an increment of added value. *Seeking Alpha*'s objective is to help its readers achieve a better return than market indices, or as they say, to "beat the market." *Seeking Alpha* generates a huge amount of data. It's not uncommon for me to receive fifty or more notices a day on stocks I follow. I don't read them all, but I do read those that seem to be particularly important to the stocks I follow. I don't use *Seeking Alpha* for investment ideas. I rarely let anything I read there form investment decisions for me. Rather, it's more like music playing in the background while I work. It's a place to hang out with folks who have similar interests.

Seeking Alpha, like the publications I recommended, gives you exposure to the language of investing and the thinking of folks who live in your new virtual neighborhood. Think of it as talking over the fence with your neighbors. All your neighbors in your new neighborhood own businesses, and that's what they talk about over the fence. You'll find *Seeking Alpha* essential to accessing data on those stocks with constantly increasing dividends. It's just a great app!

All this sounds like a lot of work and time. It isn't. Ease into the reading, and in time it will become a habit—a very good and profitable habit. A journey of discovery. New neighborhoods can be uncomfortable at first, but, in time, you'll begin to fit in.

3

THE GOAL—MAKE YOUR FAMILY RICH

REMEMBER THIS: YOUR GOAL MUST BE TO MAKE your family rich. Not just you, but your family, however you define that. It could be a conventional family of your spouse, children, and grandchildren; or it could be your nephews and nieces; or it might be a number of friends or charities that are particularly dear to you. It's the people or institutions that are likely to survive you, whose prosperity and well-being are meaningful to you, and for whom you want to provide.

You need to commit that you'll not only make them rich, but you'll also educate them in the ways to succeed you, so they can advance and sustain your wealth. This is possibly the key principle to grasping the investment strategy outlined in this book. When you make that commitment and understand why it's necessary, you'll have inoculated yourself against the crippling effects of that most devastating financial disease called retirement planning.

We all have a limited time on Earth. You can check life expectancy tables and determine the probability of living to a certain age. So can the financial planning professionals. The estimate of longevity is what informs the professional investment industry's approach to how they advise you on your investment strategy. There are entire industries whose purpose is to advise you on retirement strategies and help you implement those plans. Turn on the television, read a financial periodical, or access the internet and you'll see that financial planners and advisors are everywhere, hawking their approach and products. The tax code is designed to promote retirement, providing for all sorts of tax-advantaged Individual Retirement Account (IRA) Plans, Roth, and Keogh (no relation) Plans to insure you don't succumb to that ultimate scourge of the golden years: outliving your money.

That fellow on television always says, "The worst thing that can happen is you run out of money in your retirement." That's not the worst thing that can happen to you. Not even close. There are lots of worse things. How about a child with a drug addiction who needs rehabilitation services? How about a badly disabled, elderly spouse who needs special and expensive nursing home care? How about a grandchild struggling with some sort of learning disorder who has special education requirements available only in a private facility? You want worse? It's a long list.

If you run out of money in retirement, you'll still have Social Security, and you might even get a job, which is probably better for you than retirement. But sitting in front of the TV watching *Leave it to Beaver* reruns while a family member suffers is not where you want to be. You don't want to replay all your *wouldas* and *shouldas* as an old guy. You want to help because that's what you've always done.

I love that TV ad where the old guy has his dream car fantasy. Then his granddaughter needs help with college, and the final scene is the old fellow handing the keys to the young lady, and she says, "But, Grandpa, what about your dream car?" He responds with a smile, "This is my dream now." I love that commercial. You want to be that old guy and get your dream car too!

We said early on in this book that rich is less about buying stuff and more about independence and control of your life and your family members' lives. If you're rich, you can afford that new car, home, vacations, and dining out. New stuff can be nice too. Foremost is the independence you and your family members will enjoy because you'll have the financial capacity to smooth out all those bumps in the road of life. If you follow the precepts of this book and train your family members to manage the family's asset management business, you'll have the peace of mind an old guy wants and needs. You really don't want to face the end of Life Road with big regrets.

We regularly receive mail solicitations that invite us to lunch or dinner with financial planners and lawyers to help us plan for our retirement. Everyone seems to assume there's a time when we retire and need to save and invest with the goal of not outliving our money. That mindset implies a formula for investing that involves significant time variables. The two most important variables are 1) your retirement date and subsequent drop in income, and 2) the date on which you and your spouse are estimated to die. This approach inevitably leads to investment strategies that involve various combinations of fixed income (annuities and bonds) and equities (stocks). Typically, investment professionals see stocks as riskier than bonds, which usually leads to conclusions that exposure to stocks should decline as we progress through the golden years, while fixed income holdings should increase proportionately. That leads to various proportions like 70 percent stocks and 30 percent bonds at retirement, and maybe 40 percent stocks and 60 percent fixed income ten years later. The details from each adviser vary based on the retiree's other income sources, health, and a number of other factors. But the programs are always similar in that they trade the higher performance but uncertainty of stocks for the lower but more secure, predictable returns of bonds. You may hear about the Rule of 100. Subtract your age from one hundred, and that's the percentage of stocks you should own. For example, if you're sixty years old, your investments should consist of no more than 40 percent stocks.

> *Everyone seems to assume there's a time when we retire and need to save and invest with the goal of not outliving our money.*

Virtually all financial advisors acknowledge that American stocks outperform bonds over the long term. But, alas, none of us lives forever. "Make peace with your mortality," they say, "and let us, the financial professionals, design the formula just right for you, your age, and your longevity so you don't outlive your money." Get over that perspective and start thinking and acting so your money won't only outlive you, but continue to grow beyond your life.

No financial advisor will advise you to be completely invested in stocks. They can't. Markets can decline 30 percent or more in a few days. A financial advisor buddy told me if he advised his clients to invest the way this book recommends, in the event of a sudden 30 percent decline in market value, half of his clients would beat a path to their lawyers' offices. It's the financial advisors' lawyers who have the final say on folks' retirement plans. We advise you not to focus on the market value of your holdings but on the income those investments generate, because you're investing for your family and forever, and the value will come back in time. Despite market value, your income will increase every month or quarter.

From Retirement and Estate Planning to Succession Planning

Conventional thinking about personal financial topics focuses on retirement and estate planning. It's mostly about you and your spouse, and it's definitely based on a perception that time is limited. I bet that even Warren Buffett has a retirement and estate plan. Most of Mr. Buffett's wealth is in the stock of the company that's been his life's work, Berkshire Hathaway. Berkshire Hathaway is a huge conglomerate of diverse businesses accumulated by Buffett over his long life of investing.

While Berkshire Hathaway doesn't have a retirement or estate plan, like all well-run companies, it does have a succession plan. The succession plan is based on the presumption that the company will exist indefinitely. That is, the company will survive the demise of Mr. Buffett and those who immediately succeed him. It's not co-incidental that Mr. Buffett, when asked the ideal holding time for investments, says it's "forever." One of Mr. Buffett's primary roles, particularly at this stage of his life, is to put in place a management succession plan and to groom people to provide the leadership for Berkshire after he leaves and goes into forever. He's providing the succession plan for Berkshire Hathaway, which controls most of his personal and family wealth.

I sometimes half-jokingly refer to retirement as the great un-employment con job initiated by FDR. Confronting a devastating national unemployment rate of 25 percent during the Great Depres-sion, President Franklin D. Roosevelt created the concept of Social Security to improve his numbers. With the government-guaranteed income from Social Security, older folks were no longer unemployed but retired and off the rolls. I don't think it's natural or healthy for someone to be educated, work through their adult life, and then retire into their more advanced years at a time when they've ac-cumulated the most knowledge and experience. Some folks have physically demanding jobs or limitations and disabilities as they age, and it may be necessary for them to move on from conventional employment.

In corporations, CEOs often move on from their very de-manding jobs to less consuming roles as chairman, board director, consultant, or the like. Or they may simply be active in a role as stockholder in their former employer's company. Such transitions are usually good for the individual and productive for the enterprise because they keep an experienced hand involved in the future oversight and operations of the company.

It's not just major corporations that have succession plans. Think about family businesses like restaurants and farms. Future generations often work in the business from an early age. They may start by doing minor manual labor on the farm like mucking out stalls or washing dishes in the restaurant. They learn the business from the ground up and, in time, given the opportunity and education, may bring better, more modern skills to the business than the parents and grandparents who founded and nurtured the enterprise.

But the senior members of the family have a wealth of hands-on experience that can complement the younger generation's energy, industry, and more modern education. In many family farms, restaurants, and other businesses, multiple generations work together in changing roles over time with the overall objective of sustaining and advancing the family's well-being.

> *This book suggests a strategy to abandon the notion of a conventional retirement and most of the investment strategies that implies.*

This book suggests a strategy to abandon the notion of a conventional retirement and most of the investment strategies that implies. Our method builds upon a concept of lifetime saving and details how to think of investments as the family business, much like the multigenerational approach to a family farm or restaurant business. In addition to whatever job you have, you'll also be employed by your family's asset management business. For now, your job will be to work at your current employment, save, and build your asset management business. In building the asset management business, you'll have to plan for succession. That succession plan will be specific for your family, just as it's specific for every corporation. In general terms, it will require you to ensure that the next generation of leadership fully understands your unique asset management business and acquires the education and skills to continue to manage and grow the family asset management business.

I will detail the investment strategy of my family's asset management business and how it evolved and continues to evolve. I think our strategy may work for your family. Accepting that it's your purpose to make your *family* rich, rather than *yourself*, is key. It's an altruistic goal, but essential from a time or investment duration perspective. It's especially important because it helps you abandon conventional time restraints that actually limit your wealth-building potential by tying your hands to a limited time frame and conventional thinking and planning about your retirement. It's helpful to strike the idea of retirement from your thinking because adopting the concepts and systems we present makes retirement irrelevant. It truly is a preventable disease.

You Can Take It with You

You know that old saying, "You can't take it with you." Like many such sayings that survive across generations, it's certainly true. But using that expression to guide your financial practices can mislead you into spending now because your time is limited. I've heard my contemporaries say things like, "I'd like to die with a zero balance in my account." But if your objective is to make your family rich, then current expenditures—and particularly unnecessary spending—could deprive your family of the security and wealth you've pledged to provide.

When you commit to making your family rich, it not only dispels the conventional investment strategies defined by the standard retirement objective, it creates a time frame that survives you.

When you commit to making your family rich, it not only dispels the conventional investment strategies defined by the standard retirement objective, it creates a time frame that survives you. That's particularly important because it opens you to forever strategies of investment. In a way, you create the vehicle to take it with you, a way for you and your money to go on together. Just as Berkshire Hathaway will survive the earthly life of Mr. Buffett, your asset management business will live on after you, not only in the things you acquired, but in the skills you nurtured among your family members.

4

GO LONG ON AMERICA AND ONLY AMERICA

THERE ARE APPROXIMATELY 45,000 PUBLIC companies around the world—companies in which you can buy stock on a public exchange. Only about 4,500 of those are listed on US exchanges. So, if you buy stock only in American public companies, you can buy stock in only about 10 percent of the public companies in the world. Why invest only in American companies? If understanding 4,500 companies in any depth is impossible, then understanding 45,000 companies is *crazy* impossible. That's one reason to stick with American stocks, but it's not the most crucial one.

My Parents Were Great Investors

People occasionally ask me where I learned to invest and where I got interested in and skilled at investing and actively managing our family's assets. The answer I give is, "From my parents." But when I go into the details, they react with a mixture of surprise and amusement.

My parents were immigrants who came to this country with virtually nothing. They were truly zero-denominator folks. You might see that as the standard immigrant story. However, my parents were different in an historically important way. They chose to come to America during the Great Depression. They hadn't known each other in the old country, and they each made the same independent decision to immigrate to the US about the same time. Nothing much novel there either. But the Great Depression was the only time in US history when more people left this country than immigrated to it.

I've been to their birth places several times and visited with our extended family there. It's beautiful and the people are wonderful, but they aren't Americans, and the way they live isn't like in America. The natives and my relatives who still live there lack the energy, industry, and optimism we have in the United States.

My mother and father scraped up the money to visit the old country after they'd lived in the US about twenty years. I'd just finished the fourth grade, and they took my younger brother and me with them. My parents still looked and sounded like all the locals there, but I remember our family and their neighbors referred to my mom and dad as "the Americans." They were different from the natives, and I could see the contrast even then. The expression that best describes this phenomenon is, "The ones with the get-up-and-go got up and went."

In the old country, children tend to die in the same economic class as their forebears. My parents were among the hardest working people I've ever known. They must have realized America offered the best opportunities for their future and the future of their family. After that trip, I understood my parents differed from their countrymen. They were born with American industry and optimism; they just weren't born in America. My parents instilled in me the objective to make my family rich. I learned it by their example. That's what they did for me and my siblings.

> *My parents instilled in me the objective to make my family rich.*
> *I learned it by their example.*

My parents never bought a stock or even a house or a car. I believe they made one major, enormously successful investment that helped make their family successful and rich. Specifically, they went long on America and short on Europe at a time when most investors did the opposite. Other immigrants to the US were selling (emigrating) on that big market dip that was the Great Depression. The ones who left were traders. My folks were investors. In investment terms, my mother and father were contrarian investors, and all their progeny are thankful for that one big trade.

Whenever I returned from a visit to the old country, I never failed to tell my parents how much I enjoyed my visit and how grateful I was for their one very big, very smart trade. It must have been tough for them, but their sacrifice made life so much more successful and prosperous for their family. They did okay, and they got to see their children and grandchildren benefit greatly from their trade. Mom and Pop made that one great investment in the greatest growing dividend-generating investment of all times: America.

My parents enjoyed steady dividends over their lives. Let me give you just one example. In 1961, I was a college freshman who lived at home and commuted to school. That year, my older brother, Mike, returned to the Bronx with his young family from Indiana, where he'd earned a PhD in chemistry from Purdue. Mike was the first in our family to graduate from college and the first to live outside the New York City area. He'd taken a job with Union Carbide in New Jersey, and he stopped to see his family on the way to his new home.

We were superintendents in an apartment building in the Bronx, and I remember my father asked Mike how much he'd make in his first professional job. Mike said his annual salary was $13,500.

I'd helped my father do his income tax return and knew that amount was double what he earned in a year. At that time, the old man was fifty-seven and had worked for over forty years. Here was his son at twenty-four, just starting out, making twice his income! Talk about dividends on that one great investment!

No family member in the old country had graduated from college, much less earned a PhD. All three of my parents' sons went on to earn advanced degrees from prominent universities. The dividends to my parents just kept coming from that one great dividend-generating investment: America!

Remember the book and movie *The Big Short* about the 2007-2008 mortgage crisis that led to the Great Recession? Well, my parents did the "Big Long" on America. You should too.

Global Investing the American Way

Conventional investment philosophy says we should think globally about where to invest. It's clearly a global economy with relatively slow-growth, mature economies like the US and faster growing economies like some of those identified as emerging markets. The pros call them EMs. Some investors and financial advisors seem to have a hare-and-tortoise view of global economics. In their minds, the most successful economies, like the US, are now consigned to slower, tortoise-like growth because of their former success. The emerging market hares, on the other hand, are unencumbered by the restraints of the economics of large numbers.

Let me apologize in advance for what some may perceive as xenophobic, nationalistic views. I've travelled to many regions of the world, and I don't trust any of the places I've visited nearly as much as I trust the United States.

Let me apologize in advance for what some may perceive as xenophobic, nationalistic views. I've travelled to many regions of the world, and I don't trust any of the places I've visited nearly as much as I trust the United States. The growth rate in China may be much faster than the US, but do you really want to invest in a communist country where the government centrally controls the major industries? Sure, they can make that work for a while, but in the end it's a government-controlled communist country. Most folks now seem to agree that the Chinese government is active in routinely stealing intellectual property from the US and other countries' companies. Does it make sense to invest in a country whose practice is to steal?

When you hear that the US growth rate in gross domestic product is about 3 percent per year and China's is 8 percent to 10 percent, investing in China seems to make sense. But remember, these numbers are generated by a government that's communist and steals. Does it make sense to believe anything they say or the data they generate?

The other day I read about Jack Ma, founder and chairman of Alibaba. He's been a member of the Communist Party since the 1980s. You know what that means? No? Neither do I. But it can't be good if you're thinking about investing in BABA.

I've been to China and visited a number of its major cities. I loved China, the Chinese people, and their national monuments, but I couldn't breathe the air, and I have no interest in going back. I returned from my trip sick, and I think it had a lot to do with the air quality. If I don't want to go back, what sense does it make for me to send my investment dollars there?

Many of the most successful Chinese people immigrate to the US or Canada at their first opportunity. They send their children to US universities because they don't trust their own educational system.

Some years ago, we rented an apartment in the Washington DC area to a Shanghai real estate developer, his wife, and two daughters. This guy planned to commute between Washington and Shanghai, mostly because he wanted his daughters to be educated in the US. (I think his decision also involved his having too many children of the "wrong" sex.) The two daughters spoke perfect English, but their parents didn't, so the twelve-year-old translated for her parents as we negotiated the lease. Where do you think those young ladies will want to live, work, and raise their families? Does it make sense that some professional financial advisor thinks I should invest my money in a country where the growth rate is higher than in the US, but its own people don't seem to have confidence in their institutions? Should I believe a growth rate reported by a communist government?

What about India? I've never traveled there and have little desire to go, but it's touted as fast growing too, right? That's a country where a whole class of people are labeled untouchables. Think about that! The US Bureau of Labor Statistics doesn't compile or certify India's economic growth data. Some Indian government agency does that. Should I trust the data that comes from a government that tolerates its people being untouchable? Everywhere I look in America there seem to be well-educated, prosperous Indians. They even call it the "Indian diaspora." Why should I invest in India when her own people are leaving and investing in the US?

Then there was my trip to South America and its emerging markets. When I visited Buenos Aires, Argentina, I became a regular and very satisfied customer of the Bank of Ernie. Ernie, the founder and only employee of his eponymous bank, was an Argentinian who'd immigrated to Los Angeles and had been deported for undisclosed indiscretions. He was trying to accumulate enough capital to return to LA by whatever means available. The Bank of Ernie had a unique business strategy tailored to its Argentine domi-

MAKE YOUR FAMILY RICH • 43

cile and banking location. That is, the branch bank for the Bank of Ernie was outside a Greek restaurant where Ernie, with menus in hand, hawked the cuisine within.

Whenever Ernie engaged a dining prospect in conversation and determined his or her country of origin, he was quick to introduce the customer to the broader services offered by the Bank of Ernie: his currency exchange product. Ernie was big on cross selling his mostly foreign customers. Come for the souvlaki and leave with the local currency! At the time, the official exchange rate in Argentina was nine pesos to our gringo dollar. The Bank of Ernie offered an exchange rate of thirteen pesos for that very same dollar. For those doubting Tomasitos, the Bank of Ernie had a one-hundred-dollar introductory offer.

I took Ernie up on his special and bought 1,300 Argentine pesos to see if our hotel would accept them, and they did! From that day forward, while in Buenos Aires, I was a regular customer at the Bank of Ernie. Now think about that. Go to a real bank and get nine pesos per dollar or patronize the Bank of Ernie and get almost 50 percent more in the local currency. The food was great, and the people were nice, but do I really want to invest there?

Then there was our Buenos Aires bus trip with a local tour guide. His running description of sites and events around this beautiful city had a consistent theme. The tour could have been billed as "You Think This Place Is Screwed Up Now? You Should Have Seen It Before!" The tour agenda consisted of a litany of corruption in all things Buenos Aires, from payoffs to disappearing and murdered citizens. So, given this was the opportunity to put his city's best foot forward, it became almost comically clear that our guide thought there was nothing but bad stuff in this place, albeit better than before.

There was even one quaint artistic section of town where the guide made it clear that if we came back there on our own for some shopping, it would be necessary to leave by 6:00 p.m. because that's when the police left the area. The reason the police left, he explained, was because that's when the criminals took over. You'd think with criminals aplenty, that's where the police would and should be, right? Not in Buenos Aires! Apparently, some unwritten pact existed between the government and the criminals that 6:00 p.m. was the time to change the guard, so to speak.

I should invest in a place like that to take advantage of an emerging market? I should believe any data generated by a government where the police abandon their citizens to criminals on a schedule? Places like that can do their emerging without benefit of my capital.

Years ago on a trip to Mexico, I sat next to Boris on the plane. Boris was born to Russian Jewish parents and had immigrated to Mexico as a child with his family. As a young man, he founded a bank with his brother. While he was on a business trip in California, he received a call from his brother to notify him that the Mexican government had just nationalized their bank. The government took this guy's life work, and a year later they still hadn't compensated him.

Speaking of Russia—isn't that still a communist country? They did "privatize" a number of industries, but didn't the government make favorable deals with their friends to create oligarchs? Oligarchs aren't guys like Zuckerberg or Bezos. They're just buddies of the president. And don't those guys buy castles in England and penthouses in New York to provide a safe harbor when the inevitable catastrophe comes to their homeland? What's the catastrophe? Who knows, but isn't the current president accused of rigging elections and offing his critics? So, is Russia a place where I should invest my family's money?

You think a place like Canada is different? Please. I know it's hard to find a Canadian you don't like. Isn't it really more about them being a people you *can't* dislike? Being inoffensive is a major Canadian attribute. There are plenty of Americans you can dislike.

We describe them as ugly Americans. Heck, some folks think we elected a president on the basis of campaign promises to be the ugly-American-in-chief.

But Canada is still part of the British Commonwealth and recognizes a foreign, unelected queen as their head of state. What sense does that make? It helps to remember that Britain is not only ruled by a monarch, but one of their legislative bodies is called the House of Lords. It's not even the House of Lords and Ladies, just Lords! Can you imagine if our House of Representatives was called the House of Guys or the House of Gentlemen? In Britain, these are guys born into the peerage (Google it) who get paid to show up in powdered wigs. I understand the special relationship the US has with Britain, and I'm good with that, but don't get me started on the Brits. Canada chooses to be part of that thing.

Canada is a country with a significant French population. Historically, the Brits and French have had a bad habit of warring with each other. Remember, these two did the Hundred Years War. Maybe they were after the Guinness Record in the Crazy War Duration category. And they wonder why French Canadians cling to their language and culture and don't assimilate so well. Then there's the fact that we've invaded these folks twice in our history, and they resisted and stuck with the queen. You just can't help some people.

Speaking of the French—back in France, they're now working on their fifth republic. We're still dealing with our first. The French work a thirty-five-hour week and take off the entire month of August. They probably aspire to a thirty-hour week and a summer-long vacation. France has the highest tax rates in Europe, and I read somewhere that proportionately more millionaires now emigrate from France than any other country. *Vive la France!* But invest there? *S'il vous plaît!*

By the way, I don't think Australia is much different. Now, how do you dislike an Australian? These folks have been on our side in more wars than any other country. But I'm surprised at how uncomfortable they feel by their place in the world. I mean that geographically. It seems as if most Australians would be much more content if they were closer to the mother country. They just don't think of Australia as a country that should be that close to Asia. I think that's why many Australians constantly travel. You bump into them everywhere around the world.

Whoever came up with this British Commonwealth thing was a genius. It keeps the empire's states in some kind of obeisance to the crown. A British queen is still their head of state, and she gets to tour the empire in her yacht, and her subjects worldwide get to do their curtsy dip. Hail, Britannia! I don't think our founders would have fallen for the Commonwealth scam.

How can you be a real country with a foreign monarch as your head of state? The Australians continue to reject at the polls the opportunity to become a republic. By the way, that's the same crown that made a deal with their European neighbors to emulate the United States by creating a European Union. Now her majesty wants out of that deal by way of something called Brexit, and those same European neighbors are just a bit resistant to her majesty's exit entreaties. That whole EU deal just seems to me to be some bad news time-sharing hoax. Looks great in the beginning and easy to get into, but impossible to get out.

I'm of Irish descent, so you might think that's the reason for the British bashing. As an American, I do appreciate the special relationship, but both my parents were born in what is now the Republic of Ireland, then occupied by the Brits. Both of their birth certificates say they were born a British subject. Both parents told my siblings and me that when they wanted to emigrate, their families told them to "never go to a country that flies the Union Jack."

That whole royalty thing is all very quaint and appeals to many Americans, but our founders lost their taste for it and committed in the final sentence of our Declaration of Independence to "pledge to each other our Lives, our Fortunes, and our Sacred Honor" to part company with His Majesty and all his Lords. If Washington, Jefferson, and Adams were financial advisors today, they'd probably counsel you to go long on America and only America.

Someone soon will tell you that Cuba is a great place to invest. The story will be that Cuba is desperate for infrastructure investment, only ninety miles from the greatest markets in the world, inexpensive labor, etc. What a great frontier market and three crops a year! But it's communist. So is China, and look at all the wealth created there in recent generations. That's what those financial advisors who promote a global investment strategy will likely pitch

On a day-long tour of Havana, my mind kept turning to Taglit-Birthright Israel. *Taglit* means "discover" in Hebrew, and Jews have this thing about sending their youngsters to Israel to better understand their heritage. In Cuba, I had this overwhelming sense that we Americans need to send the likes of Alexandria Ocasio-Cortez and the growing numbers of our socialist-leaning young folks to Cuba. Maybe Bernardito Sanders would chaperone the tour. In Havana, it looks as if all progress stopped in 1959, and nothing has worked well since. The signs of Cuba's prerevolution wealth are apparent in its grand but now badly deteriorating monumental structures.

Everything in Cuba is controlled by the government. Our tour guide was a government employee, the restaurant we had lunch in was owned by the government, and the entertainment was a four-piece government-provided salsa band.

From each according to his ability and to each according to his need. That's the definition of socialism many people learned in school. Sounds good. Our guide proudly told us health care is free and is the largest industry in Cuba. In fact, the government apparently mandates one doctor per 160 citizens. But in a country where doctors earn about eighty-five dollars per month and tourists are advised to bring their own toilet paper, would you have confidence in anything? Cuba is a BYOTP country that's ninety miles from our borders!

It's not all bad news. There are some green shoots of private enterprise and property rights in Cuba. For example, our tour guide noted the problem with the city's overflowing trash cans. It seems the trash people are assigned trash trucks that frequently don't work. The truck operators then take it on themselves to fix the trucks, often with parts from their relatives in places like the Bronx. Search as you might, there don't seem to be any O'Reilly's Auto Parts in this tropical revolutionary paradise. Having restored the trucks to operating condition, the employees then think of them as *their* vehicles. With that sense of private property, they apparently feel emboldened to use the trucks for family trips to the countryside and beach, thereby neglecting their trash-collecting duties. Why do their state employers put up with this neglect of duty? Apparently, any attempt to separate the employee from his truck is met with threats to remove his parts, thereby remanding said trash truck to its previously inoperable state. Our guide presented all this in a reasoned way, as though explaining some interesting cultural adaptation.

If ever there was a place to prove you don't make the poor rich by making the rich poor, it has to be Cuba. Members of Ms. AOC's "tippy top" wealthy class are nowhere to be found. The revolution took care of that by creating a truly egalitarian system for the country. Everyone seems equally miserable in their poverty.

If you're a real estate guy, you can see enormous opportunity everywhere you look. Those fabulous heritage buildings desperately need to be repurposed and renovated, and idle labor seems to be abundant. All that's needed is capital and a rule of law to safeguard property rights. But who in their right mind would invest in a communist system? With the dissolution of the Soviet Union, Cuba lost its big brother. Our guide suggested that the only remaining source of credit is China. No surprise there.

Returning from Cuba, I had an even deeper regard for our founding generation. They created our constitutional form of government, our rule of law, and an economic system that's the foundation for our enormous prosperity. Each of us has a responsibility to preserve those things and pass them on to those who come after us. Need inspiration? Visit Cuba and bring a couple of our young socialists with you. If you like the future of Cuba, maybe you should think about investing in Kimberly Clark Corp. KMB has increased its dividend for forty-six years and produces toilet paper.

I could go on. For example, a recent *Wall Street Journal* article had a story on the Iraq stock market. Yep, Iraq has a stock exchange. It was up 10 percent in the first quarter! That's the Iraq where IEDs are a driving hazard. By the way, IED is not a trading symbol.

Whatever Happened to Political Risk?

Years ago, investors spoke of investing in other countries as fraught with political risk. It was openly discussed and evaluated. You hardly ever hear about political risk today. It's almost as though it's not politically correct. Does anyone want to be considered a *Canadaphobe*? Then how do you sell that emerging market Exchange-Traded Fund (ETF) if you think like me?

Color me an ugly American, at least economically speaking. I'm okay with that. I think I understand the risks of investing in the United States and the risks of investing elsewhere, and I limit my investments to the United States. I occasionally make an exception, as I discuss in chapter 9, but it's rare. And when I lose money venturing abroad, I chalk it up as tuition for my continuing investment education.

I think I understand the risks of investing in the United States and the risks of investing elsewhere, and I limit my investments to the United States.

There are much better ways to invest globally. Lots of people in all those emerging, developing and frontier markets eat hamburgers, drink soda, smoke cigarettes, use smart phones, brush their teeth, and wash their clothes. In fact, by confining your investment to American-based, run, and regulated businesses, you'll inevitably and much more safely get significant global exposure. Your money need not travel abroad to capture global growth. In fact, about 40 percent of revenues for the firms listed in the Standard and Poors 500 come from outside the US. By confining your investment to US-based companies, you may be exposed to some different risks—like the risks involved in currency exchange—but compared to the political and business risks elsewhere in the world, that's not a big deal to me.

To make the "investing in American companies is investing in the world" point, let's look at a couple of major American companies whose names you'll recognize. They sell stuff many of us use regularly. They also sell stuff bought by our friends around the world. Let's start with that most American of companies, McDonalds (MCD). One in eight working Americans will work for MCD at some time in their life, and 66 percent of McDonald's sales come from abroad. McDonalds sells a lot of Coca Cola (KO). Foreign sales comprise about 53 percent of KO's total revenue. Colgate Palmolive (CL) generates about 80 percent of its sales outside the US. Johnson and Johnson's (JNJ) foreign sales amount to 48 percent of their total. Then there's Procter and Gamble (PG), with 55 percent of sales from abroad. These pillars of American commerce will give you exposure to emerging markets and the higher growth rates in some areas of the world, and by investing in these American stalwarts, you'll get international diversification. And if one of the crazier countries in this world goes under, as Venezuela is desperately trying to do at this writing, then your business may suffer a bit but not that much.

So, jettison your instincts for political correctness and recognize that trying to understand multiple countries and thousands of foreign companies is neither practical nor desirable. In the investment strategy detailed in this book, the number of companies you'll invest in is more manageable, understandable, have global exposure and is, well, all-American. I really like that, and I think Mom and Pop would too. That's how they invested.

5

HOW TO AVOID THE GNU EFFECT

EVERY FINANCIAL OR INVESTMENT ADVISOR seems to have taken the same class. They all say that your best long-term investment strategy is to invest in common equities or stocks. Things get complicated when they inevitably factor in your age and a retirement perspective. Virtually all investment advisors design their strategies to accommodate your age. They do this because, as one investment advisor on TV says, "The worst thing that can happen is to run out of money before you die."

There's that crazy retirement thing again. Everyone presumes you plan to retire, stop earning, and sit back and live off your investments. Well that's not going to happen, because your job to make your family rich will never end. Your role may evolve over time, and you'll love your changing role. Because you work for your assets, they can never fire you. It's a lifetime of fulfilling employment.

Why do investment advisers worry about your age? It's because stocks can be volatile. Pity the poor investor entirely in stocks when the stock market tanks, the advisor believes. In that case, what does the standard investment advisor counsel his clients to do? Most say that as you age and approach retirement, you should gradually move more of your investments from stocks to fixed income investments like bonds. There are fixed income devices other than bonds, but, for the most part, fixed income is about bonds.

Why do they do that? Because the value of and income from bonds is more predictable and dependable. That's what they mean when they say bonds are less volatile. Over time, the returns from bonds will be less, but you can depend on them. Also, given stocks' volatility in value, the financial advisor's attorney will never let a financial advisor put you entirely in stocks.

Most corporate bonds come in one-thousand-dollar denominations and have a fixed term. That is, at some point in ten, twenty, or thirty years, they'll mature, and the principal amount of the bond will be paid to you. Usually, the longer the duration of the bonds, the higher the coupon or stated interest rate. But the longer the duration, the more the interest rate risk. Market interest rates fluctuate over time, and, generally, as interest rates rise, the market value of a bond decreases. So, values can change, but you'll receive the interest—which is the coupon or stated rate on the principal—every six months. Most corporate bonds pay interest at six-month intervals, and then at maturity you get the full face value back. Simple? Not really. There are books written about fixed income investing, but this is not one of them. We won't recommend bonds as a way to make your family rich. When you think of bond investing, try to remember them as fixed-income investments. Fixed is not a good thing.

Back to that standard investment manager. As you age, he or she recommends that you gradually migrate to a higher concentration of bonds so you can sleep well at night. There's even an acronym every financial advisor knows: SWAN. With SWANs you supposedly are less likely to run out of money before you die. You'll routinely hear advice that you need a fifty-fifty portfolio at retirement—50 percent bonds and 50 percent stocks. Then, say ten years into retirement, your portfolio should be sixty-forty, moving more into bonds. You get the picture. It mostly means you'll sacrifice the higher overall returns they tell you the equities market will generate over time for the reliability and stability of bond investments.

> *None of that applies to*
> *the guy whose objective is to make his family rich.*

None of that applies to the guy whose objective is to make his family rich. First, he's never going to retire, because when he quits his regular job, he's going to work full time, or however much time he wants, for his assets. Second, he's never going to die, or at least his death becomes irrelevant from the standpoint of his investment strategy because he's not investing for himself but for his family. He is just a collateral beneficiary. He's investing forever because his family will be forever, right?

We promote the idea that you should always be 100 percent invested in equities. Now, every lawyer for investment advisors will tell you that's irresponsible. That's because we all know there are times when the market collapses and much of your investment gets wiped out. Right? Long-term investors like Warren Buffett and I know well that the value of your portfolio can quickly decline by as much as 40 to 50 percent in a matter of a couple of years. We also know it comes back. But does it come back for the particular stocks you own? Or does it matter to you because you panicked and sold some or all of your holdings when the market tanked? You've heard all that stuff about being fearful when others are greedy and greedy when others are fearful. Great advice, and accurate too, but try acting on it when the market precipitously drops 40 percent, and you're looking at a reduced value in your account month after month.

The most likely outcome is the standard investor will be fearful when others are fearful. It's the way of nature. Ever see those video clips of the huge herd of gnus out there on the Serengeti when the pack of hungry lions makes the scene? The gnus take off lickety-split and in the same direction until they fall off a cliff or drown trying to cross a raging river. That one guy who's a bit slower becomes the lions' lunch. Our DNA, natural selection, survival-of-the-fittest thing seems to destine each of us to boogie in the same direction as everyone else at the first scent of danger. Well, we ain't gnus, and market downturns are not predatory lions, and that cliff or raging river is not the inevitable outcome.

No matter how firmly sold you are on the investment philosophy in this book, you'll never see a major market downturn as an opportunity from any position other than hindsight. Looking back, everyone has 20/20 vision, and so will you. The boxing champ Mike Tyson might have said it best: "Everyone has a plan until they get punched in the mouth." During the downturn, you'll be upset, your confidence will be shaken, and you may even panic. You'll want to burn this book and its author. Don't worry; I won't take it personally. But you shouldn't sell, and we believe there are features of our investment philosophy that will help you resist the temptation to run with the herd when that sense of panic is in the air. Most importantly, during those inevitable market collapses when your investment value declines, your income will go up!

Invest Only in Dividend Champions

There's a class of stocks commonly referred to as Dividend Aristocrats or Dividend Champions that we recommend as the foundation of your investment strategy. In fact, we recommend that you invest exclusively in this class of stock. For most people, no matter how sold they become on this approach, that won't happen. They just have other interests and expertise. From time to time, they'll have to scratch an itch or invest in things for which they have a special urge. That's okay. Just don't do too much of it. We'll discuss that in later chapters.

Dividend Aristocrat (DA) is a term used to describe firms in the Standard and Poors 500 that have paid increasing dividends in each of the last twenty-five years or longer. Dividend Champion (DC) includes all the stocks that have paid increasing dividends for that time, including those in the S&P 500. Dividend Aristocrats include about fifty-seven companies, while Dividend Champions total one hundred and thirty-nine at the time of this writing. They're all American-listed equities. I'll use DC to describe the full class of firms paying increasing dividends for over twenty-five years.

You can access the list of DAs on a number of websites. I use www.suredividend.com, developed and maintained by Ben Reynolds and his Sure Dividend Team. The DC list is available on www.dripinvesting.org, originally developed and maintained by a fellow named David Fish. Unfortunately, David died in 2018, and Justin Law assumed the job. Both David and Justin are national treasures in my view. I remember the TV show *Wall Street Week with Louis Rukeyser* and his Hall of Fame. I think of Lou as the founding father of business television. In 1970, he created *Wall Street Week* on NPR as the first entertaining, informative investment program. Each year he added to his *Wall Street Week* Hall of Fame. Some of those names include Abby Joseph Cohen, Lazlo Birinyi, Peter Lynch, and Bob Stovall. I can still see AJC interviewed in *Barron's*, and I met Sam Stovall, Bob's son, at the 2019 annual meeting of AAII. Sam told me, "Pop is still at it at ninety." If there ever is a *Make Your Family Rich* Hall of Fame, David and Justin will be the first inductees.

The DC list is more inclusive and detailed than the DA list thanks to Justin Law. You can delve as deeply as you feel comfortable. There are a couple of differences between the two lists. All the suredividend.com companies are included in the dripinvesting.org list, but suredividend has three companies not included in the dripinvesting list. Those companies are AbbVie Inc (ABBV), Abbott Laboratories (ABT), and Cardinal Heath (CAH). I asked David some years ago about the difference, and he told me that those who maintain the S&P DA list are very reluctant to ever remove a stock. ABBV was a spin-off from ABT, and that confused things, as neither company in its current state has a twenty-five-year record of dividend growth. He was less clear about CAH, simply saying that it hadn't met his very specific annual increase standard. I have all the companies on my list, so I have a total of 139 companies.

Let's understand DCs a bit more and learn how we deal with them. At the end of this chapter, you'll find a list of all current Dividend Champions and the duration of their dividend increases. Justin's list has much more data, and my list is abridged to summarize only some of the data from Justin's spreadsheet. It's an impressive list, and the reader will easily recognize many of the names. In fact, you likely are a customer of many of these firms, even if you don't know it.

> *Investing in DCs gives you a sense of ownership in the company and in America.*

Investing in DCs gives you a sense of ownership in the company and in America. At least it does for me. I love to eat at Mc Donald's (MCD has forty-four years of increasing dividends). There, I always get the bottomless senior Coca Cola (KO has fifty-seven years of increasing dividends) and promptly and reliably connect to their AT&T-provided Wi-Fi (T has thirty-five years of increasing dividends). Before settling in to lunch, I use the sanitary wipes from the convenient Ecolab dispenser (ECL has twenty-seven years of increasing dividends), and afterward, the paper supplies in the bathroom provided by Kimberly Clark (KMB has paid increasing dividends for forty-seven years). When I bring my grandchildren to MCD, I regularly point out these DCs, reminding them that their family owns them all and that by being a customer at MCD, we advance our family's future and wealth. A little family wealth with those fries is a very good thing.

Remember, one in eight employed Americans will work for MCD at some point in their life. Most MCD managers are from the ranks of the crew, as are many of the franchise owners. McDonald's is more than the first rung in the country's employment ladder, as some critics suggest. It covers all the rungs in the nation's wealth ladder. Did I mention that the world's wealthiest person, Jeff Bezos, worked at MCD in his high school years? One in eight working Americans! I'm proud we're MCD investors.

As I travel the world, I always make it a point to visit the local McDonald's and marvel at the menu adaptations MCD makes to appeal to various national palates. There's nothing quite like being in a McDonald's in Paris, spending your euros to advance your American investment interests to the silent strains of "God Bless America," knowing your MCD is up 45 percent over the last year. Now that's my kind of global investing: the American way!

With DCs, as firms reach the twenty-five-year mark, Justin Law adds them to the list, and if any of them fail to increase their dividend for even one year, he drops them from the list. Once I've bought a DC, I never sell it unless it stops being a DC, and then I sell it right away. If your holdings are all DCs, think about what happens in a market downturn, even a steep decline. The value of your holdings will go down, but your income will go up. Your income will go up not only in absolute terms, but it will particularly increase in your rate of return. The declining value of your stock in the rate of return fraction is the denominator, and the dividend income is the increasing numerator. The farther the market declines, the higher your rate of return. In a tanking market, you're still getting a raise. What effect do you expect this will have on your inevitable urge to sell in a downdraft? For us, and I hope for you, it will diminish and hopefully eliminate the urge to act like all those gnus. To resist the urge to sell is the key. Stick to the plan even when you get punched in the mouth.

Think of this in terms of your job. If you work long enough and in various fields for different companies, at some point the company you work for will run into some problems and the value of the business may go down. It might even go down a lot. You could get concerned about your future with the company and be tempted to look for employment elsewhere. But what happens if, despite the steep downturns, you keep getting raises? That's reassuring, and your incentive to change jobs probably diminishes.

That's how investing in DCs works. You'll take out your brokerage statements in times of uncertainty and check the declining value of your portfolio. But in a column nearby, you'll see your estimated annual income, and that will increase month after month. That increasing income will help remind you that you're a forever investor. The family members who come after you will be grateful for your perseverance, and so will you, because next month, quarter, or year, the value will start to recover and your income will be even greater. We say start to recover for a reason. When there's been a sharp drop in the market, stocks rarely recover at the same pace as they decline. There's an expression for that: "Markets take an elevator down and an escalator up." That's just the way it is. Think of it as Ms. Market testing your true devotion.

Trader vs. Investor

You'll frequently hear investors debate whether they're investors or traders. Traders typically are those guys who tend to be technical analysts of stocks and markets. They often rely on charts to determine patterns of trading and pricing. They purport to understand when there are bull and bear markets or tout they can see them coming. When you listen to them, you'll hear a lot about "heads and shoulders," "double tops," and the like.

If you follow the advice of this book, you should consider your-self an investor in America's best and most sustainable businesses. There will be ups and downs because the businesses you invest in won't be immune to the business cycle. One or more of your busi-nesses may run into a particular problem. A product may be re-called for a safety issue, and your stock price takes a hit. Or one of your businesses introduces a major new product, and it doesn't sell. But your DC companies have had those problems over the years, and they've worked through them and continued to give raises to their owners for at least twenty-five years. You're an investor in solid, long-term, successful businesses.

Of course, someone might get into a DC or some other in-vestment and get a quick pop over a short time and then sell. It will happen, and you'll hear about it. Folks tend to tout their trading successes and conceal their failures. Look, if you have the urge to trade short-term on a particular stock that's not a DC, go ahead and do it, scratch the itch, but don't do a lot of it. Over time, you'll see it doesn't work. But even then, if you do it in moderation, it will work for you as tuition. That's because we learn from our mistakes. You'll learn to stick with DCs when you pay the tuition for the course.

In the great trader versus investor debate, if you follow our recommendations, you'll be a proud investor in great American companies that take care of their owners. Because that's what you are. You're an owner. As you buy and promote the products of the companies you own, you should take pride in your ownership. Your sponsorship advances your family's economic interests. It should feel good to you when you brush with Colgate (CL has given its owners a raise for fifty-five years.) You won't get the same feeling from owning a mutual fund or ETF that you think may own CL. Nor will you get that same lift if you own CL and plan to sell it tomorrow because it's declined for a couple of days and you heard some expert technical guru on TV say, "CL is fully priced," or, "over bought." You're sticking with Colgate because your managers at CL are loyal to you as an owner. It's your company, your managers, and your toothpaste.

Take a look at the business cycle chart again from chapter 1. It shows you why resisting the urge to sell is so important. That chart generally depicts my life experience over more than fifty years of investing. Assets—whether stocks, real estate, classic cars, or collector art—tend to decline during recessions. Recessions are usually defined as two successive quarters of a reduction in gross domestic product. In recessions, folks tend to lose their jobs, curtail their spending, and generally take on a negative attitude toward the future and investing. Though the timing of recessions is uncertain, their occurrence is not. Recessions will happen.

But just as recessions are inevitable, so are recoveries. However, the timing of the recovery is no more predictable than the recession itself. Over twenty-five or so years, we usually have a couple of recessions. Things get rough in recessions, but the DCs have actually increased their distributions in dividends to their owners despite and during recessions. These are the companies that have withstood the test of time and the downdrafts in the business cycle. These are your guys; they have staying power, and they have your back.

Now, reflect on the Great Recession. That's the period roughly from 2008 to 2011 or so. The economy and markets tanked, but even during that time, the DCs increased their dividends. They didn't just maintain the dividends, they increased them. Why? Because those DCs, managers, and workers love their shareholders. That's why it's called the Great Recession, because during that trying time, the DCs showed their shareholders how great they really are. Remember, today's DCs also survived the bursting of the tech bubble at the end of the last century and gave their shareholders raises throughout that downturn.

Think again about the way a guy like Warren Buffett responds when asked how the market will perform tomorrow or in the coming week or year. He always says that he has no idea what will happen in the short term. But over the long term, he says, you'll always do best in equities. I think he's simply confirming what my experience has shown: the market will go down, and often it will go down a lot, but, inevitably, it will come back and come back higher than its previous high. Not everything will come back, and certainly not everything will come back to new highs. The inferior companies will stay down, some may even go out of business, but I believe DCs will come back higher and better because they always have. Remember that old adage, "Nothing succeeds like success." That works in life, in the stock market, and investing as a general rule.

There are some really smart guys out there who'll tell you there's a whole lot easier way to invest in DCs. There are a number of Exchange-Traded Funds (ETFs) that track the performance of dividend growth stocks such as the Dividend Aristocrats. ETFs trade like stocks on the exchanges and generally track the performance of an index, in our case the S&P Dividend Aristocrat Index. NOBL, for example, is the trading symbol for the Proshares S&P 500 Dividend Aristocrat ETF. There's also SDY, the symbol for the SPDR S&P Dividend ETF.

Let's take the description of NOBL: "Eighty percent of its assets are invested in securities of the S&P Dividend Aristocrat Index and comparable securities that have economic characteristics that are substantially identical to the economic characteristics of the securities in the index." Sounds like something written by a lawyer, right? What's with the 80 percent and the comparable securities stuff? Do you feel any love there?

We don't like ETFs, and here's why. Say you really like football. You're a Giants, Redskins, or Packers fan, am I right? You're not an NFL fan. What sense would "Go, NFL" make? It wouldn't! That's what buying ETFs is like. You don't want to do that. You belong to the teams of those individual businesses you own. Businesses committed to their owners through thick and thin—those are the teams you root for.

Like I've said, I love McDonald's. I like being a customer and love owning the stock. I bring the grandchildren there, and I enjoy interacting with the employees. *How's business? When's the McRib coming back? How come the salads are never on special with my app?* It's my business. Why wouldn't I want to know?

But I think MCD could be better. For example, with all the choices I get at MCD, why can't I get a whole wheat bun with those great artisan hamburgers? So, I write to the president and VP of shareholder relations about that. I tell them I get the whole wheat option at all my favorite sub shops; why not MCD?

NOBL also owns MCD. What would I do in that situation? Write to Mr. NOBL regarding my whole wheat bun issue? It would be like writing to Mr. NFL about some concern I have with the Giants. How would you get your children and grandchildren excited about an ETF? A key feature of the Make Your Family Rich approach is engaging the next generations.

On a recent flight, I noticed for the first time that there were vehicles at the airport with the ABM Industries Inc. logo. We'd just bought some ABM (paid increasing dividends for fifty-two years!). Were there always ABM vehicles and personnel providing airport facilities services, or did I just start noticing them now that ABM is our company? I don't know, but I kept a close eye on my new guys.

Investing in DCs is about owning businesses and your relationship with your businesses. MCD is an obvious example, but think about having that special relationship with your toothpaste (CL), your household cleaning agents (CLX), your drug store (WBA), and your band-aids (JNJ). We recently moved our prescriptions from CVS to WBA when we first invested in Walgreens (WBA). CVS was a bit more convenient, and I like their blood pressure machine better, but WBA is now one of our businesses. Now, I write to the president of Walgreens about improving their blood pressure machine. Incidentally, all the mailing addresses for your businesses are in the Value Line review for each company.

Dividend Growth Stocks Outperform

I don't like to compare the performance of dividend growth stocks like DCs to other investment alternatives. I prefer you think about the advantages of DC investing in a less quantitative, more common-sense way. But a recent email from the American Association of Individual Investors caught my eye. The average annual market return on dividend-paying stocks since 1926 is 10 percent per year, compared to 5.8 percent for non-dividend stocks. That's just dividend-paying stocks, not increasing dividend stocks. The email went on to say that over the past forty years, stocks with increasing dividends have significantly outperformed all other classes of stocks, whether they pay a fixed dividend, no dividend, or cut dividends.

The following summarizes some of the advantages of dividend-paying stocks and DCs in particular:

1. They provide a steady stream of income to either reinvest or use.
2. They generate higher long-term returns than non-dividend -paying stocks.
3. They offer owners a way to access cash without having to sell their stock.
4. They provide an inflation hedge, especially in the case of DCs.
5. They make your holdings less volatile than non-dividend stocks. Dividends provide something of a safety net in a down market.
6. They create greater credibility in the business's earnings. Dividends say corporate management has confidence in their current and future profitability.

The *Make Your Family Rich* program involves concentrating on DCs. Investors need to keep an eye on additions and deletions to the list of DCs. As the list expands, add to your holdings, and when companies drop off, sell. Otherwise, never sell. We'll discuss how to buy in the next chapter.

DIVIDEND CHAMPIONS
Data Courtesy of Justin Law

COMPANY NAME	TICKER SYMBOL	INDUSTRY	YEARS
ABM Industries Inc.	ABM	Commercial Services & Supplies	53
Archer Daniels Midland	ADM	Food Products	45
Automatic Data Proc.	ADP	IT Services	44
AFLAC Inc.	AFL	Insurance	37
Albemarle Corp.	ALB	Chemicals	25
A.O. Smith Corp.	AOS	Building Products	26
Air Products & Chem.	APD	Chemicals	38
Arrow Financial Corp.	AROW	Banks	26
Artesian Resources	ARTNA	Water Utilities	27
Atmos Energy	ATO	Gas Utilities	36
AptarGroup Inc.	ATR	Containers & Packaging	26
American States Water	AWR	Water Utilities	65
BancFirst Corp. OK	BANF	Banks	26
Becton Dickinson & Co.	BDX	Health Care Equipment & Supplies	48
Franklin Resources	BEN	Capital Markets	40
Brown-Forman Class B	BF-B	Beverages	36
Black Hills Corp.	BKH	Multi-Utilities	49
Badger Meter Inc.	BMI	Electronic Equipmnt & Instruments	27
Brady Corp.	BRC	Commercial Services & Supplies	34
Brown & Brown Inc.	BRO	Insurance	26
Caterpillar Inc.	CAT	Machinery	26
Chubb Limited	CB	Insurance	26
Commerce Bancshares	CBSH	Banks	51
Community Bank System	CBU	Banks	28
Cullen/Frost Bankers	CFR	Banks	26
Cincinnati Financial	CINF	Insurance	59
Colgate-Palmolive Co.	CL	Household Products	56
Clorox Company	CLX	Household Products	42
Canadian National Railway	CNI	Road & Rail	25
Chesapeake Financial Shares	CPKF	Banks	28
Carlisle Companies	CSL	Industrial Conglomerates	43
Computer Services Inc.	CSVI	IT Services	48
Cintas Corp.	CTAS	Commercial Services & Supplies	37
Community Trust Banc.	CTBI	Banks	39
Chevron Corp.	CVX	Oil, Gas & Consumable Fuels	33
California Water Service	CWT	Water Utilities	53
Donaldson Company	DCI	Machinery	33
Dover Corp.	DOV	Machinery	64
Enterprise Bancorp Inc.	EBTC	Banks	26

DIVIDEND CHAMPIONS
Data Courtesy of Justin Law

COMPANY NAME	TICKER SYMBOL	INDUSTRY	YEARS
Ecolab Inc.	ECL	Chemicals	28
Consolidated Edison	ED	Multi-Utilities	46
Eagle Financial Services	EFSI	Banks	33
Emerson Electric	EMR	Electrical Equipment	63
Erie Indemnity Company	ERIE	Insurance	30
Essex Property Trust	ESS	Equity Real Estate Investment Trusts	25
Eaton Vance Corp.	EV	Capital Markets	39
Expeditors International	EXPD	Air Freight & Logistics	25
Franklin Electric Co.	FELE	Machinery	28
Farmers & Merchants Bancorp	FMCB	Banks	57
Federal Realty Inv. Trust	FRT	Equity Real Estate Investment Trusts	52
H.B. Fuller Company	FUL	Chemicals	50
General Dynamics	GD	Aerospace & Defense	28
Genuine Parts Co.	GPC	Distributors	63
Gorman-Rupp Company	GRC	Machinery	47
W.W. Grainger Inc.	GWW	Trading Companies & Distributors	48
Helmerich & Payne Inc.	HP	Energy Equipment & Services	47
Hormel Foods Corp.	HRL	Food Products	53
Illinois Tool Works	ITW	Machinery	45
Jack Henry & Associates	JKHY	IT Services	29
Johnson & Johnson	JNJ	Pharmaceuticals	57
John Wiley & Sons Inc.	JW-A	Media	26
Kimberly-Clark Corp.	KMB	Household Products	48
Coca-Cola Company	KO	Beverages	57
Lancaster Colony Corp.	LANC	Food Products	57
Lincoln Electric Holdings	LECO	Machinery	25
Leggett & Platt Inc.	LEG	Household Durables	48
Linde Plc	LIN	Chemicals	26
Lowe's Companies	LOW	Specialty Retail	57
Matthews International	MATW	Commercial Services & Supplies	25
McDonald's Corp.	MCD	Hotels, Restaurants & Leisure	44
Mercury General Corp.	MCY	Insurance	33
Meredith Corp.	MDP	Media	26
Medtronic plc	MDT	Health Care Equipment & Supplies	42
MDU Resources	MDU	Multi-Utilities	28
MGE Energy Inc.	MGEE	Electric Utilities	44
McGrath Rentcorp	MGRC	Commercial Services & Supplies	27
McCormick & Co.	MKC	Food Products	33
3M Company	MMM	Industrial Conglomerates	61

DIVIDEND CHAMPIONS
Data Courtesy of Justin Law

COMPANY NAME	TICKER SYMBOL	INDUSTRY	YEARS
Altria Group Inc.	MO	Tobacco	50
MSA Safety Inc.	MSA	Commercial Services & Supplies	48
Middlesex Water Co.	MSEX	Water Utilities	47
NACCO Industries	NC	Oil, Gas & Consumable Fuels	34
Nordson Corp.	NDSN	Machinery	56
NextEra Energy Inc.	NEE	Electric Utilities	25
National Fuel Gas	NFG	Gas Utilities	49
Northeast Indiana Bancorp	NIDB	Thrifts & Mortgage Finance	25
National Retail Properties	NNN	Equity Real Estate Investment Trusts	30
Nucor Corp.	NUE	Metals & Mining	47
Northwest Natural Gas	NWN	Gas Utilities	64
Realty Income Corp.	O	Equity Real Estate Investment Trusts	27
Old Republic International	ORI	Insurance	38
People's United Financial	PBCT	Banks	27
PepsiCo Inc.	PEP	Beverages	47
Procter & Gamble Co.	PG	Household Products	63
Parker-Hannifin Corp.	PH	Machinery	63
Pentair Ltd.	PNR	Machinery	44
PPG Industries Inc.	PPG	Chemicals	48
PSB Holdings Inc.	PSBQ	Banks	26
RLI Corp.	RLI	Insurance	44
Roper Technologies Inc.	ROP	Industrial Conglomerates	27
Ross Stores Inc.	ROST	Specialty Retail	25
RPM International Inc.	RPM	Chemicals	46
Southside Bancshares	SBSI	Banks	25
Stepan Company	SCL	Chemicals	52
SEI Investments Company	SEIC	Capital Markets	29
Sherwin-Williams Co.	SHW	Chemicals	41
SJW Corp.	SJW	Water Utilities	53
Tanger Factory Outlet Centers	SKT	Equity Real Estate Investment Trusts	27
Sonoco Products Co.	SON	Containers & Packaging	37
S&P Global Inc.	SPGI	Capital Markets	47
1st Source Corp.	SRCE	Banks	32
Stanley Black & Decker	SWK	Machinery	52
Stryker Corp.	SYK	Health Care Equipment & Supplies	27
Sysco Corp.	SYY	Food & Staples Retailing	50
AT&T Inc.	T	Diversified Telecommunication Services	36
Telephone & Data Sys.	TDS	Wireless Telecommunication Services	45
Target Corp.	TGT	Multiline Retail	52

DIVIDEND CHAMPIONS
Data Courtesy of Justin Law

COMPANY NAME	TICKER SYMBOL	INDUSTRY	YEARS
First Financial Corp.	THFF	Banks	31
Tompkins Financial Corp.	TMP	Banks	33
Tennant Company	TNC	Machinery	48
Tootsie Roll Industries	TR	Food Products	52
Thomson Reuters Corp.	TRI	Capital Markets	26
T. Rowe Price Group	TROW	Capital Markets	33
Calvin B. Taylor Bankshares Inc.	TYCB	Banks	30
Urstadt Biddle Properties	UBA	Equity Real Estate Investment Trusts	26
United Bankshares Inc.	UBSI	Banks	45
UGI Corp.	UGI	Gas Utilities	32
Universal Health Realty Trust	UHT	Equity Real Estate Investment Trusts	34
UMB Financial Corp.	UMBF	Banks	28
United Technologies	UTX	Aerospace & Defense	26
Universal Corp.	UVV	Tobacco	48
VF Corp.	VFC	Textiles, Apparel & Luxury Goods	47
Westamerica Bancorp	WABC	Banks	28
Walgreens Boots Alliance Inc.	WBA	Food & Staples Retailing	44
Weyco Group Inc.	WEYS	Distributors	38
Wal-Mart Inc.	WMT	Food & Staples Retailing	46
West Pharmaceutical Services	WST	Health Care Equipment & Supplies	27
Aqua America Inc.	WTR	Water Utilities	27
ExxonMobil Corp.	XOM	Oil, Gas & Consumable Fuels	37

6

WHEN, HOW, AND HOW MUCH TO BUY

THIS CHAPTER MAY SEEM A BIT COMPLEX. THERE will be some math. Believe me when I tell you that it will seem confusing at first, but with some reflection, it will all become routine, almost like a habit—a good habit.

The chapter will also deal with trading stock options. Did you just have a heart palpitation? Are you saying to yourself, "I knew it! These guys are just like all these other investment types. It all made sense up to now, and then they slip it in. Options? Do they think I'm nuts?" Anyone involved in stock investing knows that options are often the route to ruin. They're complex, confusing, and all major financial problems seem to involve options trading. Right? No, not the way we're going to use them. And when you understand our use, you'll wonder why everyone doesn't invest this way. So, stick with us through this chapter, and you'll be happy you did.

Our buying rules are rigid in some ways. You already know we think you should restrict yourself to investing in DCs. These are mostly blue-chip companies that are pillars of the US economy. We understand folks want a bit of variety in their lives, so we advise you to scratch that itch if you have it, but don't do it too much. Similarly, we don't tell you how to evaluate various DC choices. We simply advise that you keep an eye on which DCs dip a lot on any given day and target those for acquisition. If you have a sense that another DC might have an advantage in a particular market, then go ahead and buy that one. You really can't go too far wrong if you confine yourself to DCs. If a particular DC has a lower dividend rate, it likely has a higher annual rate of dividend increase. Similarly, a high-priced DC, as measured by indicators like price-to-earnings ratios, is probably currently in a favored segment with a higher growth rate.

Investing in Your Business

I propose an investment strategy that's based on your buying an interest in valuable businesses. These will become your businesses. Your language and how you think about your investments are very important. You should never think of yourself or your investing as playing the market. Just the thought of that commonly used expression makes me cringe. Your investing is not a game. You're investing in serious businesses, and you're involved for the long run—ideally, forever.

> *I propose an investment strategy that's based on your buying an interest in valuable businesses. These will become your businesses.*

As a consumer, you'll be motivated to buy the products of your businesses and advise others about the advantages of working with your businesses. You're not gambling by investing in the stock market. Rather, you're buying a share in various businesses just as if you owned an interest in the corner hardware store. The vocabulary you use and the habits you develop inform the way you think and act about your investments. This is serious stuff. That doesn't mean you can't enjoy implementing the investment strategies I recommend. You can, but it will be the kind of enjoyment you get from a job well done rather than the fun you might have at an amusement park.

When should you buy DCs? The answer is really quite simple. There's never a bad time. If you believe, as I do, that markets are relatively efficient, with prices generally reflecting all the data available in the market, then high-quality stocks like DCs are always a good deal. If the market goes down a lot, DCs will almost always go down too. Not as much, maybe, but they will go down. Not to worry. Just as the market will eventually come back to a higher level, so will the DCs, at least as long as they keep paying increasing dividends. If you have difficulty understanding that line of reasoning, you might want to reread chapter 1.

At times, some DCs are better deals than others. Some days, folks overreact to news. Maybe external world events destabilize markets and individual stocks. If you watch cable business news, you'll see experts interviewed and asked, "Why did X stock rise or fall so much today?" The "expert" will opine on a Federal Reserve action, a Russian invasion of someplace or another, departure of an executive, a presidential tweet, or an increase in unemployment. There's always something to explain the drop. It may all seem to make sense in the moment, and if it's seen as bad news, the gnus will sell and prices will fall. If it's good news, the herd will buy, and prices will generally rise. The gnus buy on good news, and they sell on bad. That's what gnus do.

It's very easy to say you should do the opposite: buy on bad news and sell on good. Forget that sell part, because I've bought only DCs, and I hold them forever because I'm investing to make our family rich, and our family is forever.

That brings us down to the simpler question: when to buy. I buy when DCs dip. I maintain a list of all DCs on *Yahoo Finance*

Watchlist and, on most days, I review the list and sort the 139 or so stocks in the order of greatest declines. I do that simply by clicking on percent change to give me the list starting with the largest decrease at the moment. I focus on the top ten or so as my targets to buy. The logic is simple. DCs generally tend to be less volatile than stocks, so if a particular DC drops a lot, then it's likely a particularly good time to buy. Simple enough.

But this is where it gets a bit tricky. It may not be fully clear until you've made a couple of trades, but when the light goes on in your head, what follows will make great sense. And when that light goes on, you'll ask, "Why doesn't everyone do this?" When that happens, you'll know that you get it.

Say you check your *Yahoo* list and see that XYZ, a DC that closed yesterday (say June 20) at $50, is down 5 percent right now to $47.50. In fact, at minus 5 percent, it's the largest decliner of all DCs listed on your *Yahoo Watchlist* at the present time. Should you buy XYZ? Probably. It's a DC with over twenty-five years of increasing dividend income, and it's highly likely to give another dividend raise next year and in each of the years that follow. Imagine how much your grandchildren will earn on this stock twenty years from now with an additional generation's constantly increasing dividends! Wow, are these guys lucky to have had you! So, should you pull the trigger and buy that dude? No—wait just a bit more.

What financial professionals call "beta" is generally low for DCs. Beta is a measure of volatility, and the higher the beta, the more a stock moves relative to the market. So, a beta of 2 means the stock will increase or decrease two times that of the general market. A beta of .5 means the stock will increase or decrease at about half the rate of the general market. Predictably, stocks like DCs with increasing dividends tend to be less volatile and, therefore, have lower betas. The good news is that DCs don't go down that much in a down market. The bad news is DCs often don't go up as much in an up market. But overall, DCs outperform the market over time. Remember, your time horizon is forever.

Buy DCs Only by Selling Options

Let's go back to our XYZ stock. XYZ is down to $47.50 today, and maybe you can't find a solid reason for that. Maybe the earnings reported weren't as good as analysts predicted. But what's a quarter of a year when the DC has paid increasing dividends for over twenty-five years? You've been watching XYZ for a while, and the current dip is attractive, but it's a bit scary too. Why is it down so much? Could it go lower? One way of reducing the fear and uncertainty is to place a below-market order at, say, $45. You can do that, and if it's a good deal at $47.50, it's an even better deal at $45, right? It's good to remember that you're dealing with DCs, stocks that have increased dividends for twenty-five years or more. We can't say that enough times. At $45, your return is even better than the current price of $47.50, and you'll feel safer placing that order.

Warning: this is where we introduce the notion of stock options. Let's look at the XYZ opportunity and ask a different question. With XYZ trading at $47.50 at present (let's say June 21), would you agree to buy XYZ at $45 on September 21 of this year if someone paid you $1 today to make that commitment? That is, if the price of XYZ is at $45 or below, would you agree to buy it at $45 on September 21 if I paid you $1, cash in hand, today?

Let's say that XYZ is $44.90 on September 21. Then you'd have to pay $45. That means the effective price to you is actually $44.00 ($45 minus $1 premium already paid) or about 7.4 percent lower than today's price of $47.50. The net price you pay on September 21 of $44 ($45 -$1) is also 90 cents, or 2 percent, less than the September 21 market value of $44.90. I'd take that deal! Now the price could be less than the $44.90 in the example. Markets could sustain a major downturn in the three months between the

June and September dates, and XYZ could fall below $44. Remember that even if that happens, DC prices are buffered by that twenty-five-plus years of dividend increases.

In the preceding example, I said you buy those few DCs when they dip a lot relative to other DCs. Actually, you'll be selling a put option. And what is a put option? It's your commitment to buy a stock at a particular price (called the strike price, $45 in our example) on a prescribed date (the expiration date, September 21 in our example) in the future. If you enter into that contract, you'll receive a premium (the $1 in the example), payable on the date you make the commitment (June 21 in the example). Stick with me here, and I'll give examples of the arithmetic shortly.

Let's crank up the details a bit before going farther. Options trade as contracts, which represent the right to buy or sell one hundred shares of the underlying stock. So, the $1 premium in our example is actually $100, and the strike price of $45 will actually cost $4,500 ($45 times one hundred shares) if you have to buy the stock on the expiration date.

The earlier XYZ stock example cast as a put trade would take the following form. (I'll exclude trading commissions, which we'll talk about in chapter 11.) One hundred shares of XYZ today cost $4,750 ($47.50 x 100 shares). A September 20 put premium with a strike price of $45 ($4,500 for the 100-share contract) priced at $1 will yield $100. Technically, that would be called an out-of-the-money put. This is a put where the strike price is lower than the current market price.

The moment you enter that order and it's accepted, the $100 will show up in your account. Got that? Go buy lunch for a couple of buddies and sell some of our books. You just earned $100 for agreeing to buy a DC that's selling for $47.50 today for $45 three months from now. In this book, we'll discuss mostly selling out-of-the-money or at-the-money puts. An at-the-money put is one in which the current market price is identical to the strike price. That would be $47.50 in our example. An at-the-money put would typically sell for a premium higher than an out-of-the-money put. In our example, a September 20 put with a strike of $47.50 might garner a premium of $2 or more, resulting in a net stock purchase price should you have to buy the stock at $45.50 ($47.50 - $2). So, if your put strikes, you'll be buying the stock at a net cost of $2 less than the price on the day it took a big dip.

Cash-Backed Puts

Now let's look at the effects of this put sale. If you decide to be a cash-backed put seller, you'll need to reserve $4,500 cash in your account. A cash-backed put is one in which you've reserved sufficient cash in your account to buy the stock if, on the expiration date, the market price is below the strike. For making that commitment, you'll earn $100, for an annual yield of about 8.8 percent. That's $100 ÷ $4,500 = 2.2 percent. Because the $4,500 is committed for about three months (until September 21), the return is four times the 2.2 percent, or 8.8 percent on an annual basis. Of course, the actual rate should be computed on a daily basis, counting the precise number of days from the commitment to the expiration date and then multiplying by 365, but 8.8 percent is close enough for illustration purposes here.

Earning 8.8 percent is not bad, and returns on out-of-the-money put sales are often greater than that. In chapter 10, we'll discuss the higher yields available if you're able and willing to sell puts with the potential to incur debt. We call those kinds of trades margin-backed puts. The risks are a bit higher, but there are ways to manage those risks.

If the price on September 20 is over $45, then the option simply expires. You keep the $100, and your $4,500 is freed up. When we say you keep the $100, we are simply emphasizing that you already have the $100 premium and that can't ever be taken back. If the market price is below $45, then you bought the stock for the strike price at the end of the expiration date. In our example, that price was $45, or a total investment of $4,500. Remember that your net cost is really the $4,500 strike less the $100 premium, or $4,400. In the end, you don't lose value in the short term unless the market price at option expiration is $44 or less.

Here's the worst that can happen in that scenario. When this DC drops a lot to $47.50, you decide you'll buy that stock three months forward at $45, and you receive a $100 cash payment to make that commitment. If it doesn't drop below $45, you made $100, or 8.8 percent annualized. If it goes below $45, it actually has to fall below $44 before your trade loses value. Even in that instance, your income is likely to increase from the point you made your decision, and your rate of return on the lower cost will be even higher than it would have been on the day you decided to sell the put. Remember, that was the day when this particular DC dropped a lot.

There's one hard and fast rule in selling puts. Never, never, never sell a put on a stock you don't want to own. Of course, you want to own any and all of the DCs, so if you follow our program, you'll only sell puts on DCs.

That won't be practical for some folks. In fact, it's not practical for most folks. They may have knowledge in a specific field or a particular stock and will have the urge to periodically venture out into other stocks. It's just human nature. You may love all things Apple (AAPL). You've used the iPhone for years, and you have the latest Apple watch, and you just love to pay for your Big Mac (MCD with forty-four years of increasing dividends) and your Coke (KO with increasing dividends for fifty-seven years) with Apple Pay on your watch. Hey, we understand. Go ahead and add AAPL to your *Yahoo Finance Watchlist* and maybe sell an out-of-the-money put when AAPL dips a lot. We'll cover that more in the chapter 9. It's okay to scratch the itch, but don't do it often or a lot.

Here are some more details on put selling. Remember, you'll only be *selling* puts, never *buying*. Just as with stocks, there's a bid and an ask price stated per contract. The bid price is the price someone is offering to pay you to make the commitment to buy in the future. The ask is the best price someone is currently asking to make that commitment. Depending mostly on the size of the company, the bid-ask spread will be narrower or wider. A large company like a Dividend Aristocrat, whose stock trades in large volume, will typically have a more active options market and a narrower spread. A smaller company will have less trading in the stock and usually thinner trading in options and a wider bid-ask spread. As with stocks, you can always place a market offer, in which case you'll sell the put at the then bid price. Market bids can be a bit dangerous because something could happen, and the bid price could drop precipitously by the time your offer hits the market.

I prefer to look at the current bid and ask, as well as the most recent sale. I usually place my ask price slightly below the current ask. What happens then is either the fellow making the market has to sell at my ask or adjust the stated ask to my offered ask. I typically trade in smaller lots of one to four contracts, so the market maker, if he wants to keep his stated ask, will have to accept my offer or change the ask price for everyone. He or she might not want to have a smallish offer like mine drive the market, so he might be tempted to take my offer. There usually are only a matter of pennies involved in larger issues, but those pennies add up and may be enough to pay for my trading commission.

On thinly traded issues, it's not uncommon to see a bid of seventy cents and an ask of $5.00, with a last sale of $1.00. In that case, if I really want to pursue the stock, I might offer $4.50 or so. Then, I keep an eye on the ask price during the day and nudge it down depending on how the options and stock trade. I prefer larger issues with tighter spreads of a nickel or so. That way, I have reasonable confidence that my ask will hit some time during the day.

As in the stock market, you can make offers for the day, or good until cancelled. I always make day offers. Too much can happen overnight to leave offers open into the next day.

Many options expire on the third Friday of each month. More heavily traded options can have more frequent weekly expirations. The farther out in time you go, the higher the premium. I rarely go out farther than three months and never longer than four months. Things just get a bit too uncertain for my taste beyond that point. Believe me, the longer dated options are tempting, given the relatively high premiums. I just get uncomfortable going longer than three or four months. Much longer expirations could get a whole lot more volatile, and I'd hate to buy the optioned stock at significantly lower prices than the then market. But again, if you just need to grab that high premium on a long-dated option, go ahead and scratch the itch, but don't do a lot of it.

Resistance to Selling Puts

I've met many investors who understand the math and language of put selling. They're true believers in the advantages of such an investment approach. Why wouldn't they be? You get current income for a commitment to buy a favored stock for less than today's market price. For cash-backed puts, you usually get good returns on the cash you set aside. I've met relatively few investors who've actually traded options. I don't know exactly why, but I think of it as a disconnect between the investor's head and his or her finger. They just can't click the mouse to make that trade.

Experienced stock investors, even those who understand the math, have intuitive trouble with the language of options.

Experienced stock investors, even those who understand the math, have intuitive trouble with the language of options. You will too, at first. You'll be buying stock by a process of selling a put. Technically, you sell to open, and if you want to later reverse the transaction, you buy to close. When you sell to open, it's not now, it's sometime in the future when you may buy the stock. Then there is the *Make Your Family Rich* idea of selling the dips. Investors are used to being urged to buy stocks on dips. We recommend that investors sell puts on dips as the best way to invest in stocks. It's confusing, particularly to those experienced in stock investing, because the language of trading seems to have different meaning when applied to options trading. But with some experience, selling puts can become routine.

I frequently read and hear comments from investors on blogs like *Seeking Alpha* who say, "XYZ Company is down a lot. I would back up the truck if XYZ ever dropped to my target price of $45." When you tell them that they can collect $100 today to make that commitment, they simply don't get it. Or they do get it but have the head-to-finger disconnect and can't make the trade. I don't think there's a better way to buy stocks you want to own. You get current income and may eventually buy DCs at prices lower than current prices. Sell the dips. Just keep saying that to yourself. Savor it and let it sink in.

It will help to practice a bit before you finalize your put trades. You will probably make an occasional mistake. Everyone does. For example, you buy a put instead of selling one. Or you scratch your itch and sell a put on a non-DC that you're sure is at rock bottom, and it goes down further. When you make a mistake or wander off the system, reverse the transaction and think of the loss as tuition. You need to periodically pay tuition for the refresher course on sticking with DCs. When your put selling becomes routine, it will seem as simple as entering an order to buy a stock. Okay, I overstated that a bit, but not much. If you're an experienced stock investor, we think there will always be a part of you that's just a bit uncomfortable with buying stock by selling puts. You may always be a bit uncomfortable bidding on a put sale by entering an ask price. Your discomfort will diminish with time, but we think you might always have some trepidation.

At any given time, I may have forty to fifty put options outstanding. My broker marks them when they're at the strike price or below, so I know what my potential obligation could be on upcoming expiration dates. I keep an eye on that to make sure I don't get overextended. That said, my put sales are a wonderful source of supplemental income.

Options trading can be infinitely complex and fraught with risk. It's a bit like shopping at a huge department store. They have everything, but you can buy almost all of it somewhere else at lower prices. Let's pretend only Macy's has those socks you really like. They're expensive, but you can't find them anywhere else, so the only time you go to Macy's is to buy those great socks. We think selling puts on DCs falls into that sock category.

The Options Store is crazy complex, and there are volumes written on the mathematics and probabilities of trading options. At the Options Store, they market straddles, strangles, vertical bear put spreads, iron condors, collars, and even married puts. The products are almost endless. The *Make Your Family Rich* method of using put options to generate additional income and take advantage of market dips on DCs is a simple and lucrative way to use the options market to your advantage. You'll do so without incurring significant risk or being consumed by the intricacies and work needed to create a portfolio of options and manage options strategies. You'll simply sell puts. In the business, you're called a writer of puts. And, hey, your parents always thought you had what it takes to be a writer. They'd be so proud!

A Truly Great Strategy

In our working lives, we've all had a bit of TGIF. Friday is the end of the work week, and we have the weekend to look forward to. When you get into the business of selling puts, Fridays bring a whole new level of excitement. The third Friday of each month is when most options expire. The most heavily traded stocks and options often have weekly expirations on other Fridays during the month. Such options are conveniently called *weeklies*.

At a Friday market close, I find out which puts expire and which ones execute. The good news is, if the options expire unexecuted, I've earned the premium and don't have to buy the stock. My capital is freed up to do it again; wash, rinse, repeat. If the options result in execution, the good news is, I've bought a DC that I wanted at an even lower net price than the market price when my new DC dipped so much and I first entered the put sale. Bad news? There is none. You don't get that many win-win deals in investing, but the put selling of options on DCs on market dips just might be one of those rare win-win deals.

Steven M. Sears is a writer at *Barron's*, and in his weekly column "The Striking Price: Options" on August 5, 2019, he described put selling like this: "This is widely known among market insiders, who often refer to selling puts on blue-chip stocks—allowing the seller to pocket a premium if the underlying stock rises in value, but also committing him or her to buy the shares if their price falls—as one of the truly great strategies." That summarizes our experience. By the way, Steve's weekly column on options in *Barron's* is a good read. It might be a bit of a heavy lift at first, but everything gets lighter over time. This is a guy you want in your neighborhood. Incidentally, some years ago in an email exchange with Steve, he mentioned that much of what he knows about markets he learned from his grandmother from talking to her each day at market close. Now there's a *Make Your Family Rich* grandma!

There's one variant on TGIF. You'll be selling American put options. American puts, unlike European puts, can be exercised before the expiration date. Occasionally, the person on the other side of a put requires you to buy the stock before the expiration date. It's only happened to me relatively close to the expiration date when there's a sizable spread between the current market price and the strike price. I have an Apple put that will expire in a couple of days, and the strike price is $210 with a current market price of $193. That's an actual case, and it's for a stock that's not a DC. It's one of my scratch-the-itch" put sales. In my experience, it rarely happens with DCs because they're less volatile. In the case I cite, I think the person buying on the other side of the transaction is anxious to lock in his gain and wants to make sure I don't buy to close before the expiration date. It rarely happens that a put is exercised before it expires, but be prepared when it does.

A lot of stock investors say buying stocks isn't the hard part. They believe that knowing when to sell is the real challenge. We don't buy that, and we'll discuss the reasons why in chapter 8.

Value Line

I've read and relied on *Value Line* for years. Many libraries have the print edition and many more offer their members access to the on-line edition. At the end of this chapter, you'll find a couple of examples of *Value Line's* individual company reports for selected DCs. Right away, you'll notice that the print is so fine that you can't read it. But you can access the information in your "new neighborhood": the public library. The print reports are updated quarterly, but some data is kept more current in the online version.

From the examples, you can see that single sheet contains a lot of data on each company. *Value Line* also rates each company in three categories—timeliness, safety, and technical—on a scale of 1 to 5. The lower the number, the better the rating. For the most part, DCs tend to be in the 1 or 2 ratings for safety. There are some 3s, but even then, the stock is usually relatively safe in terms of its financial security and the predictability of its earnings and dividend. Timeliness refers to the *Value Line* analyst's view of where the stock and its industry are relative to other industries and stocks in the market. I tend to emphasize the timeliness and safety ratings and pay less attention to the technical rating, which is a more subjective measure of a stock's anticipated performance relative to the *Value Line* universe. I make some note of the technical rank, but I mostly rely upon the timeliness and safety measures.

I read the analyst's review of the stock. The write-up often gives the reader special insight into the company and any business challenges peculiar to the business.

To summarize my use of *Value Line*, I rarely buy a DC or any other stock with a safety rating below 3. I tend to be cautious of timeliness ratings below 3. But if the ratings are better (1 or 2), I may sell more puts that I would otherwise. So if XYZ shows up on my Yahoo *Finance Watchlist* as a big dipper, and the *Value Line* rating for safety is a 2 and the timeliness rating is also a 1 or 2, then I'm more likely to sell multiple puts on the issue.

Value Line is one of those publications best read in the print version. It's just a very pleasant way to spend a couple of hours in the library. As with everything in this book, the more you engage with *Value Line*, the more questions you'll ask. As you satisfy those issues, you'll become better informed and increasingly comfortable with the methods I propose. That's important for many reasons, chief among them being the confidence to avoid the gnu effect in the face of that inevitable, precipitous down market.

Remember, your market value will go down, perhaps a lot. But you're focused on income, and that will consistently go up.

Summary of the DC Investment System

Let's take this investing system out for a spin. For the sake of this example, we'll presume you've identified all the DCs and entered them into your Yahoo Finance Watchlist. You've custom designed your worksheet to include the following six data elements:

1. Trading symbol for each DC
2. Name of each company
3. Current price
4. Percent change in price from prior closing price
5. Daily price range showing low and high
6. 52-week price range showing low and high

The market has been open for about thirty minutes, so you take the following steps:

Step 1. Pull up the *Yahoo Watchlist* and notice that the XYZ Company is down 4 percent on the day. Your list tells you that XYZ is trading at $135 right now, which is close to the low for the day. That stock is about 5 percent above its 52-week low. You also note that ABC is trading at $45, near its low for the day but about 7 percent below its 52-week high.

Step 2. Go into your brokerage account and enter the trading symbols for XYZ and ABC. There, perform the following:

- Check the dividend rate and annual earnings. It's a good idea to confirm that the dividend is covered by the most recent earnings.
- Check the beta. Stocks with lower betas are preferable, and you should be particularly careful if the beta is higher than about 1.4.
- Check the portfolio to confirm how much of XYZ and ABC you already own and how many options on XYZ and ABC— and at what price and duration—are in the account.

Step 3. If you don't already know the *Value Line* ratings, check *Value Line*. The purpose here is to refresh your memory about the companies and see how comfortable you are with them. (The *Value Line* check should rarely stop you from pursuing the opportunity, but if the *Value Line* report is particularly strong, you may want to sell more put options.)

Step 4. Check the put pricing on XYZ and ABC and focus mostly on about three months out. Let's say XYZ is a heavily traded stock with monthly maturing and heavily traded options. You see that XYZ $120 strike puts three months out are bid $1.80 with an ask of $2.10, and the last sale was at $2.10. If you enter a market order, you'll get something around $1.80. Be careful about doing that. In this case, you decide to enter your ask on one contract for $2.05. If the order clears, $205 minus a modest commission will be deposited instantly to your account. If the market maker doesn't accept that ask, then he has to change the stated ask to your outstanding ask of $2.05. When the order is entered, check to see if it executed. If not, let it sit for a while and come back later to potentially change your ask.

In the case of ABC, maybe there's a particularly strong *Value Line* report, and you don't own the stock and have no outstanding puts. In this instance, you check the three-month options and see a bid on $40 strikes three months out at $0.55 bid and $0.70 ask. In that case, you might initially offer $0.67 on three contracts and see what happens. If they hit, $201 will be deposited to your account.

This common sense four-step approach earns you current income and the prospect of acquiring the stock in no more than three months at a price substantially below today's price, which has just sustained a rather significant dip.

A couple of final notes on buying DCs. If you watch the business news and read business publications as you should, you'll hear and read a lot about diversification. The idea is that spreading your investments over a broad range of industries will reduce the overall risk to your investment portfolio. The thinking is that market trends may clobber a particular industry, and if you're disproportionately invested in that industry, you'll get hurt too. You may have heard that decreasing interest rates adversely and disproportionately affect some industries such as banking, or that increasing interest rates hurt the housing industry. Conventional wisdom says that diversification will smooth out the risk of a sudden drop in your portfolio's value if you're "overweight" in a particular industry when the adverse event occurs. Simple and true enough. There are DCs in virtually every industry group. Most individual DCs will dip disproportionately to other DCs on occasion. Over time, following the system outlined in this book will naturally result in a diversified portfolio.

There are DCs in virtually every industry group.

The list of DCs at the time of this writing consists of 139 stocks. The following list will give you some indication of the diverse range of industries.

Industry Segment	Number of Firms
1. Communications Services	4
2. Consumer Discretionary	8
3. Consumer Staples	17
4. Energy	4
5. Financials	35
6. Health Care	5
7. Industrials	28
8. Information Technology	4
9. Materials	12
10. Real Estate	7
11. Utilities	15
Total	**139**

Then there's the matter of applying this system to Individual Retirement Accounts. You're permitted to sell options in an IRA, and your gains are tax deferred, depending on the kind of IRA you have. The main difference between an IRA and a taxable account is that margin accounts aren't permitted in IRAs. The advantage of trading on margin in selling puts is discussed in chapter 10.

The Other Side of the Trade

People sometimes ask me where the money comes from when I get paid to sell a put. They ask why someone would take the other side of the trade. Remember, DCs tend to be low beta, low-volatility stocks. I only sell puts when a DC goes down on a particular day. The fellow who owns that stock was likely surprised that his low-volatility stock went down so much. Some will sell, but others will want to stick it out. They might have a big gain in the stock and don't want to pay the capital gains tax on a sale. The owners may see the drop as an anomaly and think it will promptly bounce back, but they're a bit shaky from the drop and may want insurance against an even larger drop in the stock. So, they buy a put below the current price to ensure that if it drops further, they can sell the stock at that strike price. It's like an insurance premium.

If you sell puts, you're in the insurance business. You provide some guy with downside protection. It's like writing a fire policy on his home. If it burns (stock goes down), you'll cover the loss. That's what a put is, and being in the insurance business limited to DCs is a great business to be in.

As part of our succession planning, my children and I are working with a grandchild to periodically review all the Value Line reports for DCs and include the three rankings on an expanded spreadsheet of all DCs. How can you go wrong by introducing another generation to *Value Line*?

Get Help

I trade with TD Ameritrade and have for many years. They have wonderful online training sessions on options. The folks there have a deep understanding of the business, and I've found most, if not all, trade options for their own accounts.

This is just speculation on my part, but I think brokerage firms see a significant opportunity in helping their clients deal in options. Most of their clients don't currently deal in options, and the brokerage firms see a largely untapped business opportunity. Whatever the reason, we find the people at TD Ameritrade who deal with options matters extremely knowledgeable and helpful.

The TD Ameritrade software is terrific. Because we only sell puts and the occasional call, we don't use anything close to the full potential of their systems, but we do find the software excellent. The firm's personnel are happy to spend whatever time is necessary to help you become proficient. Particularly on your first couple of put trades, you may want to call in and have someone walk you through the process.

> *I make an occasional mistake. You will too.*

I make an occasional mistake. You will too. I've bought a put rather than sold it. The default on the system is buy. I get careless, the phone rings, someone comes to the door, and I enter the trade incorrectly. I get upset with myself, and I call those nice people at TD Ameritrade to make sure I reverse the trade correctly. On one occasion, they actually cancelled the trade for me. I'm not sure how they did that, and I didn't expect them to do it, but they did. I was very appreciative. That's just one of the reasons I love TD Ameritrade. Even if they don't reduce my fees to rock bottom, I'm probably not going to leave them. Make sure you don't tell them that!

There is a variant on the put-selling approach to investing in DCs. With transaction costs at zero today, a smaller investor can directly buy shares in quantities of a single or a couple of shares with no cost to make the purchase. If you buy into the *Make Your Family Rich* system, go ahead and buy a share or two of a DC on a dip

Warning: Selling puts can become addictive. Every time you click on the ask, money is deposited into your account. It feels really good! But one day the market will tank. It always does. Then you'll have to buy back those puts or buy the stock at the reduced price. If you have the cash in the account, that'll be a good thing. If you don't, you'll have to go into debt on margin. Then you'll look at your account and its reduced value, and your basic instincts will kick in. Your value may be down, but your income is up, and you'll need to remember that you keep score in a different way. At that time, that'll be easier said than done. Don't let that happen to you. Remember, you're investing in great American companies. Selling puts is a great way to do that and, coincidentally, generate some additional income. Generating income from selling puts is not the objective!

MCDONALD'S CORP. NYSE-MCD	RECENT PRICE 193.28	P/E RATIO 23.8 (Trailing: 24.6 Median: 19.0)	RELATIVE P/E RATIO 1.36	DIV'D YLD 2.6%	VALUE LINE 365

TIMELINESS	3	Lowered 5/4/18
SAFETY	1	New 7/27/90
TECHNICAL	1	Raised 11/8/19
BETA	.75	(1.00 = Market)

| | High | 67.0 | 64.8 | 80.9 | 101.0 | 102.2 | 103.7 | 103.8 | 120.2 | 132.0 | 175.8 | 190.9 | 221.9 | |
| | Low | 45.8 | 50.4 | 61.1 | 72.1 | 83.3 | 89.3 | 87.6 | 87.5 | 110.3 | 118.2 | 146.8 | 173.4 | |

LEGENDS
15.0 x "Cash Flow" p sh
- - - - Relative Price Strength
Options: Yes
Shaded area indicates recession

18-Month Target Price Range
Low-High   Midpoint (% to Mid)
$192-$281 $237 (20%)

2022-24 PROJECTIONS
	Price	Gain	Ann'l Total Return
High	240	(+25%)	8%
Low	200	(+5%)	4%

Institutional Decisions
	4Q2018	1Q2019	2Q2019
to Buy	886	899	887
to Sell	864	899	921
Hld's(000)	519901	517534	519305

Percent shares traded	24 16 8

% TOT. RETURN 10/19
	THIS STOCK	VL ARITH.* INDEX
1 yr	13.8	4.9
3 yr	88.4	30.2
5 yr	141.6	36.8

	2003	2004	2005	2006	2007	2008	2009	2010	2011	2012	2013	2014	2015	2016	2017	2018	2019	2020	© VALUE LINE PUB. LLC	22-24
Revenues per sh	13.58	15.01	16.20	17.93	19.55	21.09	21.12	22.85	26.44	27.49	28.38	28.50	28.03	30.05	28.74	27.41	28.20	29.85		36.30
"Cash Flow" per sh	2.36	2.88	2.96	3.43	4.06	4.85	5.22	5.92	6.77	6.93	7.24	6.65	6.89	7.86	8.54	10.02	10.15	10.95		13.45
Earnings per sh A	1.43	1.93	1.97	2.30	2.91	3.67	3.98	4.60	5.27	5.36	5.55	4.82	4.97	5.71	6.66	7.90	7.85	8.50		11.00
Div'ds Decl'd per sh ■	.40	.55	.67	1.00	1.50	1.63	2.05	2.26	2.53	2.87	3.12	3.28	3.44	3.61	3.83	4.19	4.72	5.00		6.25
Cap'l Spending per sh	1.04	1.12	1.27	1.45	1.67	1.92	1.81	2.03	2.67	3.04	2.85	2.68	2.00	2.22	2.33	3.57	3.00	3.05		3.05
Book Value per sh C	9.50	11.18	11.99	12.84	13.11	12.00	13.03	13.89	14.09	15.25	16.16	13.35	7.82	d2.69	d4.12	d8.16	d12.10	d13.90		d15.40
Common Shs Outst'g D	1261.9	1289.9	1263.2	1203.7	1165.3	1115.3	1076.7	1053.6	1021.4	1002.7	990.40	962.90	906.80	819.30	794.10	767.10	745.00	720.00		650.00
Avg Ann'l P/E Ratio	14.1	14.4	16.2	16.0	17.6	15.8	14.4	15.4	15.9	17.3	17.5	20.0	20.2	21.1	22.3	21.1	Bold figures are Value Line estimates			20.0
Relative P/E Ratio	.80	.76	.86	.86	.93	.95	.96	.98	1.00	1.10	.98	1.05	1.02	1.11	1.12	1.14				1.10
Avg Ann'l Div'd Yield	2.0%	2.0%	2.1%	2.7%	2.9%	2.8%	3.6%	3.2%	3.0%	3.1%	3.2%	3.4%	3.4%	3.0%	2.6%	2.5%				2.8%

CAPITAL STRUCTURE as of 9/30/19		22745	24075	27006	27567	28106	27441	25413	24622	22820	21025	21025	21500	Revenues ($mill)	23600
Total Debt $32850.1 mill Due in 5 Yrs $11805 mill		34.2%	35.6%	35.9%	35.7%	35.9%	35.0%	35.1%	39.0%	42.7%	49.5%	49.0%	49.5%	Operating Margin	51.0%
LT Debt $32850.1 mill LT Interest $1340 mill		1216.2	1276.2	1415.0	1488.5	1585.1	1645.5	1555.7	1516.5	1363.4	1482.0	1550	1600	Depreciation ($mill)	1600
(LT interest earned: 9.3x; total interest coverage: 9.3x) (135% of Cap'l)		4405.5	4961.9	5503.1	5464.8	5585.9	4757.8	4693.3	4920.2	5415.0	6205.3	6005	6290	Net Profit ($mill)	7150
Leases, Uncapitalized Annual rentals $1145 mill.		30.4%	29.3%	31.3%	32.4%	31.9%	35.5%	30.5%	31.7%	31.2%	24.1%	25.0%	26.0%	Income Tax Rate	26.0%
		19.4%	20.6%	20.4%	19.8%	19.8%	19.9%	17.3%	18.5%	20.0%	23.7%	29.5%	28.6%	29.3%	Net Profit Margin	30.3%
No Defined Benefit Pension Plan		427.6	1443.8	893.8	1519.0	1880.1	1437.6	6692.6	1380.3	2436.6	1079.7	1100	1200	Working Cap'l ($mill)	1500
Pfd Stock None		10560	11497	12134	13633	14130	14990	24122	25879	29536	31075	33500	36000	Long-Term Debt ($mill)	40000
Common Stock 753,093,326 shs.		14034	14634	14390	15294	16010	12853	7087.9	d2204	d3268	d6258	d9000	d10000	Shr. Equity ($mill)	d10000
		18.8%	19.8%	21.6%	19.8%	19.4%	18.1%	16.1%	16.1%	22.4%	27.0%	26.5%	26.5%	Return on Total Cap'l	25.5%
MARKET CAP: $146 billion (Large Cap)		31.4%	33.9%	38.2%	35.7%	34.9%	37.0%	66.2%	NMF	NMF	NMF	NMF	NMF	Return on Shr. Equity	NMF
		15.5%	17.5%	20.1%	16.8%	15.4%	12.0%	20.6%	NMF	NMF	NMF	NMF	NMF	Retained to Com Eq	NMF
		51%	49%	47%	53%	56%	68%	69%	62%	57%	52%	60%	59%	All Div'ds to Net Prof	57%

CURRENT POSITION	2017	2018	9/30/19
(MILL.)			
Cash Assets	2463.8	866.0	1177.3
Receivables	1976.2	2441.5	2005.3
Inventory (FIFO)	58.8	51.1	42.6
Other	828.4	694.6	379.7
Current Assets	5327.2	4053.2	3604.9
Accts Payable	924.8	1207.9	849.5
Debt Due	—	—	—
Other	1965.8	1765.6	3426.1
Current Liab.	2890.6	2973.5	4275.6

ANNUAL RATES	Past	Past	Est'd '16-'18
of change (per sh)	10 Yrs.	5 Yrs.	to '22-'24
Revenues	4.0%	1.0%	4.0%
"Cash Flow"	8.0%	4.5%	7.5%
Earnings	8.5%	4.5%	8.5%
Dividends	11.0%	8.5%	8.5%
Book Value	—	—	NMF

Cal- endar	QUARTERLY REVENUES ($ mill.) E				Full Year
	Mar.31	Jun.30	Sep.30	Dec.31	
2016	5903	6265	6424	6028	24621
2017	5675	6049	5754	5340	22820
2018	5139	5354	5369	5163	21025
2019	4956	5341	5431	5297	21025
2020	5050	5450	5550	5450	21500

Cal- endar	EARNINGS PER SHARE A E				Full Year
	Mar.31	Jun.30	Sep.30	Dec.31	
2016	1.23	1.45	1.62	1.43	5.71
2017	1.47	1.70	1.76	1.71	6.66
2018	1.79	1.99	2.10	1.97	7.90
2019	1.72	2.05	2.11	1.97	7.85
2020	1.90	2.15	2.30	2.15	8.50

Cal- endar	QUARTERLY DIVIDENDS PAID ■ ■				Full Year
	Mar.31	Jun.30	Sep.30	Dec.31	
2015	.85	.85	.85	.89	3.44
2016	.89	.89	.89	.94	3.61
2017	.94	.94	.94	1.01	3.83
2018	1.01	1.01	1.01	1.16	4.19
2019	1.16	1.16	1.16	1.25	

BUSINESS: McDonald's Corporation operated, franchised, or licensed 38,298 fast-food restaurants in the United States, Canada, and overseas under the McDonald's banner (as of 9/30/19). About 93% are operated by franchisees or affiliates, with the remainder under the control of the company. Foreign operations contributed 64% of systemwide sales and 54% of consolidated operating income in 2018. The company sold a stake in Pret A Manger in 2008. Spun off Chipotle Mexican Grill in 2006 and Boston Market in 2007. Has about 210,000 employees. Officers/directors own less than 1% of common stock (4/19 Proxy). CEO. Chris Kempczinski, Inc.; Delaware. Address: 110 North Carpenter Street, Chicago, Illinois 60607 Telephone: 630-623-3000. Internet: www.mcdonalds.com

McDonald's parted ways with CEO Steve Easterbrook after he was involved in a consensual relationship with an employee, thus violating company policy and showing "poor judgment." Mr. Easterbrook, who is widely credited with turning the business around with all-day breakfast and an embrace of technology, was succeeded by Chris Kempczinski, who most recently held the title president of McDonald's USA. We expect him to stay the course near term, though a new hand at the tiller always brings with it an element of uncertainty.

Third-quarter financials were weaker than expected in a few areas. The top line increased 1% from a year earlier, essentially matching our $5.430 billion forecast. However, the figure was slightly below the consensus on Wall Street. The company performed well overseas, but faced stiff competition at home. In the U.S., same-store sales rose 4.8%, bringing the global comp to 5.9%. Growth in the key U.S. market was below the Wall Street consensus of 5.2%. At home, transactions fell, but price increases and promotions drove sales. Too, earnings per share rose just a penny year to year, while our forecast was $2.17 and the consensus was about $2.21. Despite sales being on par with our call and the share count declining, total operating costs and expenses moved 66 basis points higher as a percentage of sales. Meantime, the tax rate increased 114 basis points and interest expense moved 51 basis points higher. Foreign exchange was a $0.03 headwind.

All told, it was not a bad quarter for McDonald's. Same-store sales growth was broad based, albeit weighted toward overseas markets. Management's embrace of technology to make the dining experience more enjoyable and efficient has been well received by consumers, as have its menu innovations and promotions. Fierce competition and higher costs appeared to be the main factors behind the U.S. comp and earnings misses. Looking ahead, we think the fourth quarter will bring more of the same, meaning that management will execute well but face familiar headwinds.

As for McDonald's stock, we think that it has appeal as an income vehicle for conservative investors.
Matthew Spencer, CFA   November 22, 2019

(A) Based on diluted shares. Excl. nonrecur. gain/(loss): '03, (25c); '04, (6c); '05, 3c; '06, 53c; '07, (63c); '08, 9c; '09, 13c; '10, (2c); '15, (17c), '16, (27c); '17, (29c); '18, (16c); '19.
(B) Excl. cum. effect of accting change: '03. (3c); '04, (8c). Incl. tax benefit: '04, 7c. Excl. tax benefit '05, 4c. Next egs. report due late Jan. (B) Div'ds paid mid-Mar , Jun., Sep., Dec.
■ Div'd. reinvestment plan available. (C) Incl. intang. At 12/31/18, $2,331.5 mill.; $3.04/share. (D) In mill., adj. for splits. (E) May not sum due to rounding.

Company's Financial Strength	A++
Stock's Price Stability	100
Price Growth Persistence	65
Earnings Predictability	85

Reprinted with permission of Value Line, Inc.

WALGREENS BOOTS NDQ-WBA

RECENT PRICE	58.99	
P/E RATIO	9.9 (Trailing: 9.8 / Median: 16.0)	
RELATIVE P/E RATIO	0.57	
DIV'D YLD	3.1%	

VALUE LINE

TIMELINESS 4	Lowered 5/24/19
SAFETY 2	Lowered 12/19/14
TECHNICAL 4	Raised 12/6/19
BETA .95 (1.00 = Market)	

18-Month Target Price Range
Low-High Midpoint (% to Mid)
$49-$97 $73 (25%)

2022-24 PROJECTIONS
	Price	Gain	Ann'l Total Return
High	110	(+85%)	19%
Low	80	(+35%)	11%

Institutional Decisions
	1Q2019	2Q2019	3Q2019
to Buy	617	517	501
to Sell	649	732	635
Hld's(000)	569145	549741	540789

	2003	2004	2005	2006	2007	2008	2009	2010	2011	2012	2013	2014	2015	2016	2017	2018	2019	2020	© VALUE LINE PUB. LLC 22-24	
Sales per sh A	31.72	36.65	41.16	47.04	54.24	59.68	64.07	71.83	81.17	75.88	76.29	80.38	94.91	108.36	115.46	138.15	152.86	164.70	193.55
"Cash Flow" per sh	1.47	1.72	1.99	2.30	2.74	3.03	3.02	3.37	3.93	3.59	3.99	4.33	5.35	6.21	6.99	8.15	8.45	8.80	10.60
Earnings per sh AB	1.12	1.32	1.52	1.72	2.03	2.17	2.02	2.16	2.64	2.53	2.61	2.90	3.88	4.59	5.10	6.02	5.99	6.00	8.75
Div'ds Decl'd per sh C■	.16	.18	.22	.27	.33	.40	.48	.59	.80	.95	1.14	1.28	1.37	1.46	1.53	1.64	1.78	1.88	2.35
Cap'l Spending per sh	7.02	8.04	8.67	10.04	11.20	13.01	14.54	15.34	16.70	19.32	20.55	21.63	28.32	27.59	26.83	27.31	26.97	29.70	45.80
Book Value per sh	1024.9	1023.3	1025.4	1007.9	991.14	989.18	986.56	938.61	889.29	944.06	946.60	950.39	1089.9	1083.0	1023.8	952.13	852.54	850.00	775.00
Common Shs Outst'g D	27.7	26.3	27.9	26.0	22.2	17.1	13.9	15.9	14.8	13.2	16.3	21.8	20.2	18.0	16.1	11.5	10.8		11.0
Avg Ann'l P/E Ratio	1.58	1.39	1.49	1.40	1.18	1.03	.93	1.01	.93	.84	.92	1.15	1.02	.94	.81	.62	.61		.60
Relative P/E Ratio	.5%	.5%	5%	.6%	.7%	1.1%	1.7%	1.7%	2.1%	2.8%	2.7%	2.0%	1.8%	1.8%	1.9%	2.4%	2.8%		2.5%
Avg Ann'l Div'd Yield																			

CAPITAL STRUCTURE as of 8/31/19
Total Debt $16836 mill. Due in 5 Yrs. $8654 mill.
LT Debt $11098 mill LT Interest $464.1 mill.
(31% of Cap'l)
Leases., Uncap. Annual rentals $3.5 bill.

Pension Assets-8/19 $9131 mill Oblig. $6834 mill

Pfd Stock None

Common Stock 892,541,146 shares
as of 9/30/19
MARKET CAP: $52.7 billion (Large Cap)

CURRENT POSITION	2017	2018	8/31/19
Cash Assets	3301	785	1023
Receivables	6528	6573	7226
Inventory (LIFO)	8899	9565	9333
Other	1025	923	1118
Current Assets	19753	17846	18700
Accts Payable	12594	13566	14341
Debt Due	251	1966	5738
Other	6135	5448	5690
Current Liab.	18547	21667	25769

	63335	67420	72184	71633	72217	76392	103444	117351	118214	131537	136866	140000	Sales ($mill) A	150000
	29.3%	29.7%	29.9%	30.0%	31.0%	31.3%	27.7%	27.9%	27.7%	24.8%	23.6%	23.5%	Gross Margin	26.0%
	6.7%	6.7%	7.0%	6.7%	6.8%	7.8%	5.7%	7.6%	7.7%	7.1%	6.6%	6.5%	Operating Margin	8.0%
	7496	7562	8210	8385	8582	8309	13100	12848	12822	14327	13882	14175	Number of Stores	15250
	2006.0	2134.0	2411.1	2223.8	2497.0	2798.0	4085.0	5009.0	5003.0	5989.2	5529.0	5275	Net Profit ($mill)	6850
	36.6%	36.7%	37.5%	37.0%	37.1%	36.9%	19.9%	21.5%	22.1%	17.8%	13.5%	17.5%	Income Tax Rate	20.0%
	3.2%	3.2%	3.3%	3.1%	3.5%	3.7%	3.9%	4.3%	4.7%	4.6%	4.0%	3.8%	Net Profit Margin	4.6%
	5280.0	4489.0	4239.0	2038.0	2991.0	3347.0	3100.0	8870.0	1206.0	d3821	d7069	d6500	Working Cap'l ($mill)	d2750
	2336.0	2389.0	2396.0	4073.0	4477.0	3736.0	13315	18705	12684	12431	11098	10000	Long-Term Debt ($mill)	7000
	14376	14400	14847	18236	19454	20561	30861	29980	27466	26007	24152	25250	Shr. Equity ($mill)	35500
	12.2%	13.0%	14.2%	10.2%	10.7%	11.8%	9.9%	10.9%	14.3%	16.3%	16.5%	16.0%	Return on Total Cap'l	18.5%
	14.0%	14.8%	16.2%	12.2%	12.8%	13.6%	13.2%	16.8%	20.0%	23.0%	22.9%	21.0%	Return on Shr. Equity	19.5%
	10.9%	11.1%	11.9%	7.9%	7.5%	7.8%	8.8%	11.5%	13.8%	16.3%	16.1%	14.5%	Retained to Com Eq	14.0%
	22%	25%	27%	35%	42%	43%	34%	31%	31%	29%	30%	31%	All Div'ds to Net Prof	27%

BUSINESS: Walgreens Boots Alliance, Inc. is the world's premiere drug distributor, anchored by its network of drugstores in North America and Europe. As of 8/31/19, it operated 13,882 stores across the globe, including 9,277 locations in 50 states, Puerto Rico, and the U.S. Virgin Islands. In 2019, pharmacy contributed 74% of sales (3rd party, 97.1% of Rx). Other general merchandise, 26%. Stores average $9.86 million in annual sales. Has approximately 342,000 employees. Acquired 2,186 Rite Aid stores in September, 2017. Off. & dir. own 15.7% of stock. Vanguard, 7.4%; BlackRock, Inc., 5.7% (12/18 Proxy). CEO: Stefano Pessina, Chairman: James A. Skinner Inc.; ll. Addr: 108 Wilmot Road, Deerfield, IL 60015. Tel: 847-914-2500. Internet: www.walgreens.com.

ANNUAL RATES	Past 10 Yrs.	Past 5 Yrs.	Est'd '16-'18 to '22-24
of change (per sh)			
Sales	8.5%	7.0%	8.0%
"Cash Flow"	10.0%	11.0%	10.0%
Earnings	10.0%	13.0%	9.0%
Dividends	18.0%	13.0%	7.5%
Book Value	10.5%	10.0%	9.0%

Fiscal Year Ends	QUARTERLY SALES ($ mill.) A				Full Fiscal Year
	Nov.30	Feb.28	May 31	Aug.31	
2016	29033	30184	29498	26636	117351
2017	28501	29446	30118	30149	118214
2018	30740	33021	34334	33442	131537
2019	33793	34528	34591	33954	136866
2020	34500	35150	35600	34750	140000

Fiscal Year Ends	EARNINGS PER SHARE AB				Full Fiscal Year
	Nov.30	Feb.28	May 31	Aug.31	
2016	1.03	1.31	1.16	1.07	4.59
2017	1.10	1.36	1.33	1.31	5.10
2018	1.28	1.73	1.53	1.48	6.02
2019	1.46	1.64	1.47	1.43	5.99
2020	1.40	1.60	1.52	1.48	6.00

Cal-endar	QUARTERLY DIVIDENDS PAID C ■				Full Year
	Mar.31	Jun.30	Sep.30	Dec.31	
2015	.3375	.3375	.360	.360	1.40
2016	.360	.360	.375	.375	1.46
2017	.375	.375	.400	.400	1.53
2018	.40	.40	.44	.44	1.88
2019	.44	.44	.4575	.4575	

Walgreens Boots Alliance stock is up about 20% in value since our September review, thanks in large part to speculation of a possible takeover bid. Although details are scarce, rumors are swirling that private equity firm KKR has made a bid to take the healthcare giant private with an offer believed to be in the neighborhood of $70 billion.
Going private would not be an easy task, though. Walgreens currently sports a $50 billion-plus market capitalization. Its privatization would be the largest to date, and the financing surrounding such a scenario would likely be problematic. In keeping with *Value Line* policy, we will continue to evaluate Walgreens on a stand-alone basis for now.
The company, meanwhile, continues to struggle from an operational standpoint. Sales increased just 1.5% in the fourth quarter, and earnings were down a nickel on a year-over-year basis, due to gross margin pressures stemming from a challenging reimbursement environment, among other things. (Fiscal 2019 ended August 31st). We look for earnings to remain relatively flat in fiscal 2020,

despite the likelihood of aggressive share repurchases and realization of some benefits from extensive cost-cutting endeavors. Management recently upped its targeted annual savings from the restructuring efforts to $1.8 billion by fiscal 2022. However, we don't expect significant contributions to be realized until fiscal 2021. Fiscal 2020 guidance seems to support our position, with management looking for EPS to be flat with last year, plus or minus 3%. Bottom-line growth should pick up nicely thereafter, however, thanks to an improved cost structure. Too, the company recently signed a partnership agreement that will give it access to Indonesia.
Patient accounts may want to try their hands here. The stock holds wide 18 month growth prospects and offers worthwhile 3- to 5-year total return potential. To wit, Walgreens generates strong cash flow and tends to be shareholder friendly. However, the near-term picture is not overly appealing, and the company must prove that it can deliver on its cost-cutting goals. These shares are ranked 4 (Below Average) for Timeliness.
Andre J. Costanza   December 13, 2019

(A) Fiscal year ends August 31st.
(B) Based on diluted shares. Excludes non-recurring gains (losses): '03, 2¢; '04, 1¢; '10, (4¢); '11, 30¢; '12, (11¢); '13, (5¢); '14, (90¢);
'15, 12¢; '16, (77¢), '17, ($1.32), '18, (67¢); '19, ($1.68). May not add due to rounding. Next earnings report due late Dec. (C) Dividends historically paid in March, June, Sept., and
Dec. ■ Direct stock purchase plan avail. (includes dividend reinvest.).
(D) In millions.

Company's Financial Strength	A+	
Stock's Price Stability	75	
Price Growth Persistence	55	
Earnings Predictability	95	

Reprinted with permission of Value Line, Inc.

7

DRIP, DRIP, DRIP—COMPOUND INTEREST ON STEROIDS

M Y FAVORITE DAYS AFTER OPTIONS-EXPIRATION Fridays is any day when a dividend is paid on my DCs. I just love dividend payment days. It's on those days I DRIP. Let me explain.

Let's say you've bought your first DCs. You pinched pennies to get the money together to get started. You sold a put, and on expiration day you bought the stock. Now you have those nice growing dividends coming in and you want to go out and treat your lady to an expensive dinner to celebrate how smart you are. Don't you dare! You've started your new part-time job as an asset manager, and you're on your way to making your family rich. To do that, you need to increase your assets. The market gives you a great way to do just that!

At the end of each quarter, you'll receive your quarterly dividend for each of your DCs. Dividends are almost always paid quarterly, though a select few pay at a different interval, like monthly or annually. Somewhere on your monthly account statement, there will be an Annual Income figure. This is your broker's estimate of how much income your current investment holdings will generate in the coming year. Over time, this item will increase as you accumulate DCs and their dividends go up annually or more frequently. It's like knowing you'll get a regular raise at your job. Through good times and bad times, your income will just keep increasing. Even if the value of your holdings decreases from one period to another, your income will increase.

What to do with your new income? Well, you could take the income and buy stuff. But we wouldn't advise that unless you have to. Or you might let the dividends accumulate so you can buy more DCs. We think the best approach is to DRIP those dividends. DRIP stands for Dividend Reinvestment Plan. Most folks know about the long-term magic of compounding interest rates. Returns balloon over time under the effects of compound interest accumulation. In fact, Albert Einstein said, "Compounding is mankind's greatest invention because it allows the reliable, systematic accumulation of wealth." Well, DRIPs are compound interest on steroids. If you don't currently need the dividend income, then choose to DRIP your dividends and let those dividends buy you more DCs.

> *Many corporate DRIP plans have features that sell you additional shares in amounts equivalent to your dividend distribution at a discount from the current market price.*

Many corporate DRIP plans have features that sell you additional shares in amounts equivalent to your dividend distribution at a discount from the current market price. Virtually all add shares to your account with no commission or administrative cost, so you acquire additional shares at a cost lower than what you'd pay in the market. How great is that! DRIPs are compound interest on steroids! We think DRIPing on DCs may be mankind's greatest invention.

It just doesn't get any better than opening your account statement and seeing those low-cost additional shares added to your holdings. All companies that DRIP do so in fractional shares. They add shares to your account in exactly the amount that can be bought with your dividend. If your dividend is $50 and the share price is $20 at the time the DRIP is exercised, you'll get an additional 2.5 shares.

As you may know, you can't sell fractional shares on the market. Our broker simply buys any fractional shares at the end of the day if we sell all the full shares of the stock. If we have 208.5 shares of XYZ and sell the 208 shares, the broker will buy the .5 at the end of the day.

Did we mention we just love DRIPing DCs? With DCs, not only do your dividends go up every year, but you gradually buy additional DC shares at reduced cost, and those additional shares earn at the DCs' increasing dividend rate.

With most brokerage statements, turning DRIPs on and off is easy. In our accounts, there's a button to click for DRIPs. By simply checking a box, the stock will be DRIPed. If you uncheck (perish the thought), your account will be credited the cash dividend. You can DRIP or un-DRIP any time you like.

One final point, and it's important. Even though you don't receive the cash dividend, you will still be required to report the income and pay the income taxes on your dividends. The need for cash to pay taxes might be a reason to keep some holdings un-DRIPed. But try not to do that. Better to sell some of your junk on eBay or get a second job. DRIPs are just too good a deal to pass up.

8

WHEN AND HOW TO SELL

IF YOU'VE FOLLOWED OUR PROGRAM SO FAR, THEN you own only DCs, and DCs are forever friends of yours unless they stop being DCs. That happens only if they stop increasing dividends. When that happens, you should sell. It takes something big for a company's management to interrupt over twenty-five years of increasing dividends. You don't want to stick around to find out how big that something is.

We sometimes have a different practice when it comes to scratch-the-itch stocks. Let's say you sold a put on a non-DC. It looked great. All the talking heads on CNBC went on about what a bargain the stock was at the current price. Maybe you even used the company's product and loved it and couldn't understand why the stock wouldn't go to the moon. But it didn't. It just kept going down, and you didn't want to acknowledge you had to pay tuition. I've been there with stocks like General Electric (GE). What a bargain it would be at $17, way down from its high. So, I sold some $17 puts at $0.50, and the stock closed at $15 on the expiration day. Down deep, I knew I'd made a mistake, but I convinced myself that GE still made sense, though I wasn't quite so sure. Rather than simply sell and take the loss, I sold $16 calls for another $0.50. When the calls expired, GE was at about $10. You get the picture. Today GE is at $9 and change, and I've sold calls at a constantly declining strike price. I mitigated my loss by collecting call premiums, but my loss is still greater today than if I'd simply sold the stock when it first failed to meet my expectation. I could have mitigated my loss even more by never getting involved in GE and sticking with my DCs.

> *For scratch-your-itch stocks, I think it's always best to sell when the stock doesn't perform as you expected.*

For scratch-your-itch stocks, I think it's always best to sell when the stock doesn't perform as you expected. Remember, selecting the stock was your attempt to become a stock picker. You thought you were smarter than the market. Turns out, you're not. Listen to the market when it tells you that a stock that's paid an increasing dividend for over twenty-five years is not a flash in the pan. Don't beat yourself up. Just sell and get back on board the DC train, destination Making-My-Family-Richville.

Investing in DC forever stocks helps you avoid selling anxiety. There's always someone calling for a collapse in the market or the stock(s) you own. That's what makes a market. There's almost always a buyer and a seller for any given stock. As a DC investor, you're insulated from that anxiety. You're not focused on the value of the stock as much as on the income the stock generates. Any individual stock may go down at any given time for a variety of reasons, but your investments are constantly increasing your income.

Another significant advantage of never selling your DC forever stocks is you don't pay capital gains taxes on your profits. If fact, if you hold your stock at the time of your death, the stock passes to your heirs not only tax free, but the heirs take the stock with a new basis at the time they acquire the stock from your estate. There may be an estate tax if your estate is large enough, but there will be no capital gains tax on the appreciation of value during your life.

9

SCRATCH THAT ITCH

SOME MAY FIND OUR APPROACH A BIT RIGID, MAY-
be even robotic. You know, limiting your investments to div-
idend-increasing US-based DCs and selling puts on market
dips, then DRIPing dividends as they're earned. Not a lot of deep
analysis there. What about fundamentals, market trends, technical
analysis, and that occasional Fibonacci retracement? How about the
whole exotic nature of global investing in emerging and even frontier markets? Those are the kinds of things all those smart talking
heads on CNBC and Bloomberg go on about. China's and India's
economies are growing much faster than the US. Then there are
commodities. What about investing in gold, silver, and bitcoin?

Even after you embrace our system, you'll still have doubts.
There will be times you underperform the various market indices.
But remember, every comparison involves a time frame. You're up
8 percent for the year, but the Dow Industrial Index, for example,
is up 10 percent. You underperformed, right? Not really, because
you're investing forever, so any shorter-term comparison could be
misleading or irrelevant. If you're running a marathon, who cares
who won the 100-yard dash at the start? That said, there will come
a time when you think you see a special opportunity. Each of us
seems to have a need to act independently every so often to capture

that one bright idea—to depart from the system. General Electric is at an all-time low, or the banking industry is clearly in recovery and Citibank (C) or Bank America (BAC) is selling below book value. They may even have been paying an increasing dividend for a couple of years.

What should you do? Go ahead and scratch the itch if you have to, but don't do a lot of it. Maybe limit these itch investments to 5 percent of your portfolio. That's the way we do it. Mostly, when we scratch the itch with a stock like GE, we regret the action. We sell a put on GE believing that it's unlikely to go below 15, and it does, and we buy the stock and then it goes down further. Why? Well, we think it's partly because the company hasn't created that increasing dividend safety net that's common with DCs. The same with the likes of Citigroup Inc. (C) and Bank of America Corp (BAC). They went through a particularly tough time during the Great Recession, when their stock prices collapsed and they either eliminated or reduced dividends. Dividend Champions continued to increase their dividends even during the Great Recession. In fact, there are a number of industrial firms that are DCs (but not GE), and a number of banks that are also DCs (but not C or BAC).

> *If you have to scratch your itch,*
> *we recommend you do it by selling puts.*

If you have to scratch your itch, we recommend you do it by selling puts. Then if the price declines and your confidence waivers and you want to get out of the investment, a good way to reverse your position might be to sell calls. A call is another form of option. A covered call is one kind of relatively safe call. Covered means you own the stock on which you're selling a call. Calls, like puts, trade in contracts that consist of one hundred shares. The sale of a covered call means the owner is offering to sell a contract on a per-share basis on a particular future date. If the stock price is above the strike price, then the owner will be required to sell the underlying shares.

Let's say you sold a $17 put on XYZ when the stock was selling at $18.50. Maybe you received $0.75 for that put sale. Then when XYZ hit $16 on the expiration date, you bought it for $17. You're in a loss position on the expiration date because you paid a net of $16.25 ($17 strike minus the $0.75 premium), and that position is now worth $16. Then XYZ continued to decline. When it hit $15, you'd learned your lesson and sold a $16 call for another $0.75. The stock continued to drop and was at about $14 when the $16 call expired, and you then sold $15 calls. You get the picture. You recognized your mistake, realized that you had better choices, and decided to get out of the investment. But instead of simply selling, you used the income from the call option sales to minimize your loss. Of course, the alternative is simply to recognize the mistake, chalk the loss up to tuition, and sell the stock outright.

My Scratch the Itch

I've long invested in Washington, D.C. area community banks. In fact, it's my favorite form of real estate investing because the primary asset of community banks is often mortgage loans. Washington, D.C. is one of the wealthiest areas of the country. I've also invested in the area's banks because I have extensive real estate holdings in and around that area, and I believe having bank investments helps facilitate mortgage borrowing. So, Washington community-bank investing is a variant from the Dividend Champion investment strategy. You may have something like that, and I advise you to pursue your special interest or talent, but do it very cautiously.

Typically, I buy local banks that pay a dividend. Because Washington is such a wealthy metro area, I've experienced solid growth in our investments, and because they're all smaller community banks, they also experience a great deal of merger and acquisition activity. Over the years, several of the banks have been bought out, and that generally results in a sudden increase in market value of about 20 to 30 percent. In fact, today I own none of the banks I owned ten years ago. They've all been bought out. Some were bought with cash and others at least partially with the stock of the acquiring bank. In many cases, I still own the stock of the acquiring bank and hope that an even larger bank will acquire them. That happened recently, where a community bank (Middleburg Bank) in the outer suburbs of Washington, D.C. was acquired by a closer-in bank (Access National), only to sell out to a larger Virginia bank (Union). With each sale, there was a pop in the market value of the stock. I think the trend toward larger and larger banks is inevitable, given the high cost of regulatory compliance and the advantages of scale. But there will always be new or so-called de novo banks, and as they become successful and grow, there will be larger banks that want to acquire them. It's a specialty area of investment in which I have many years of successful experience. I know the market and many of the practitioners in the business. My real estate holdings give me an additional reason to stay involved with this specialty interest and investment class.

The truth is, I'm comfortable with Washington, D.C. area community banks. You may have something like that too. If you do, you might want to make some investments in your special area of interest. But I suggest that you limit those investments. Focusing on Dividend Champion investments gives you the kind of sustainable investment strategy that will transcend any individual's interest or skills. The performance of a DC-based investment strategy will usually transcend any particular generation's special interest and skills.

10

NOT ALL DEBT IS BAD ALL THE TIME

I LIKE DEBT ON REAL ESTATE DEALS. IT SHOULD BE reasonable, relative to the value of the property and the income it generates. So, having a 60 percent or maybe a 70 percent mortgage will likely make sense. When I was younger, I carried more debt. In a way, I had to because I had a whole lot less capital than I do now, and I was anxious to make my family rich. You have to be careful, particularly with adjustable rate mortgages. A 5 percent loan today could adjust in three to five years to 7 percent and then 9 percent in another five years or so. The deal that worked at 5 percent could eat your lunch at the higher rates. I feel particularly comfortable with mortgages on residential real estate. People need a place to live, so dealing with a long-term vacancy is unlikely. Then there are the advantages of real estate loans. When a property is appreciating, your return generally increases with more debt because rate of return is measured as the return on invested capital. The less equity and more debt you have in the deal, the greater the return.

As a practical matter, most real estate investments require substantial capital, and you may not want to devote that much capital to a particular property by paying cash, so a mortgage is desirable.

One of the things I like most about mortgages is seeing my statements every month. I just love to note the amount of principal I've paid down. It's like having a friend who makes a contribution to your savings account every month. It's also a bit like seeing your dividends DRIP every quarter. Each month, I enter the new, lower loan balance on my Personal Financial Statement (PFS), which increases my net worth. For these reasons, every one of our real estate investments has a mortgage. Not big mortgages—rarely more than about 70 percent of the property's value. We're comfortable with that, and the net income from the properties easily covers the debt service.

Borrowing on Margin

Borrowing against your stock holdings is another matter. When markets are going up, you'll be tempted to borrow on margin to buy more. A margin account is one in which you're authorized to buy additional equities with funds borrowed from your broker. Interest is typically paid monthly directly from your account. Your margin balance usually may not exceed 50 percent of the value of your account. In a down market, if your margin balance exceeds the 50 percent limit, you'll have to add additional capital, or your broker is authorized to sell your stock to bring your account into compliance. Not all stocks are marginable, but virtually all DCs should be marginable.

Margin interest rates can be negotiable. The rate generally decreases as a function of the amount borrowed. That is, the higher your balance, the lower the rate. Margin is like everything else in this life: a little bit won't hurt you and may be good for your returns. Particularly in an up market with a portfolio of stocks whose dividends are constantly increasing, a margin balance can enhance your returns just as a mortgage improves real estate returns in an appreciating market. The problem is that it can be hard to control. Margin debt has a kind of narcotic effect on an investor, particularly when they experience enhanced returns in an up market. It's difficult to not continue to increase your margin balance. As we all know, an up market is inevitably followed by a down market, and a margin account has the opposite effect in a down market. The margin balance acts as an accelerant to reduce the value of your investment portfolio, and that can be anywhere from painful to disastrous.

There are some accounts in which you can't buy stocks on margin. Retirement accounts like Individual Retirement Accounts (IRAs) don't allow margin accounts. That's because of the risks involved. Regulators want investors to be especially cautious with their retirement funds.

We have to admit that we use a margin account, but for a very specific purpose and in moderate amounts relative to the overall value of our holdings. As discussed in chapter 6, we buy stock through the sale of put options. To recap, there are two basic ways to cover the contingent obligation when selling a put. By contingent obligation, you'll remember that selling a put means you're obligated to buy the underlying stock if on the expiration date the market value of the stock is at or below the strike price. A put sold with a strike price of $50 requires you to reserve $5,000 in your account to buy that stock. So, if you sell the put for $2 with a $50 strike and an expiration date three months hence, your return on the $5,000 set aside is 4 percent for the three months and 16 percent annually. Pretty good, and that's how a cash-secured put works.

Margin-Secured Puts

Now let's suppose you're fully invested in DCs and have no cash available in your account. You see a big dip in a DC on a given day, and you really want to sell a put and possibly own the stock at the strike price. You've applied for a margin account, and your broker is satisfied you have the qualifications to manage margin responsibly. Plus, you have adequate securities in your account to secure the obligation you incur should the put eventually require you to buy the underlying stock. In that case, you could sell a margin-secured put.

Here's how a margin-secured put works. Let's take the same $50 strike three months in the future. You sell the put at $2, and $200 (less commission) is immediately deposited to your account. Your broker sets aside the $5,000, reducing your margin availability by that amount. The good news is that you don't actually borrow the funds and incur an interest cost at the time you sell the put. You only borrow the funds if, on the strike date, you're required to buy the stock, and then your margin balance will be $5,000.

What happens to your returns? If the put expires unexecuted, you've earned $200 without committing your capital or incurring debt. That means your return is infinite because in the rate of return fraction, the numerator is $200 and the denominator is $0. The result is an infinite rate of return. Compare that to the terrific 16 percent return on the cash-backed put sale. Well, there's no comparison. You can't beat an infinite rate of return.

Now if a margin account in an up market can have a narcotic effect on an investor buying stocks, imagine the effect an infinite rate of return can have in selling puts. If you do sell margin-backed puts, it might be better to sell puts further out of the money or at lower strike prices. Let's say XYZ stock, a DC, has just dropped 5 percent to $150. When you check your *Yahoo Finance Watchlist*, you see that XYZ is trading near its 52-week low. Maybe you check *Value Line* and see that XYZ is rated a 3.2.3 for the timeliness, safety, and technical factors. When you look at the available options, you see that three months out there's an at-the-money $150 strike, as well as strikes at $145, $140, $135, and $5 increments lower. You don't have cash ($15,000) available to cover the put sale, but if you could get the stock at $135, you'd be willing to incur the margin debt. On offer is a $1.00 premium, or $100 for selling a $135 put three months forward. The way you might evaluate this transaction is that the probability of the put sale resulting in a stock purchase is relatively low, so it's unlikely you'll incur the margin debt. But if the put at expiration results in a $135 purchase of XYZ, you'd be satisfied—very satisfied. Maybe even more satisfying is the prospect of the put expiring above $135, and you get to keep the $100. The point is that if you're going to face the possibility of incurring margin debt, you may want to take the lower premium associated with the lower strike price.

> *You certainly shouldn't sell margin-backed puts in your early days of implementing the system in this book.*

You certainly shouldn't sell margin-backed puts in your early days of implementing the system in this book. We do use margin to sell puts, but we use it moderately and keep a watchful eye on the potential balance. We must be mindful of where our contingent liability is at any given time. You have to presume that all puts you sell will result in purchases at their strike prices and that you'll be comfortable and able to handle the resulting margin balance. You can manage the contingent liability by buying to close puts after you've made a reasonable gain. When you buy to close, you release the margin-contingent liability and take your gain on the put trade.

Buying stock or selling put options on margin is not something someone new to this form of investing should do. But as you advance and your wealth grows, you may want to consider a modest amount of margin. Because we only buy DCs by selling puts, we incurred all our outstanding margin obligation by selling margin-backed puts on DCs. There's risk, and if you choose to go this way, do so with caution and always assume the worst.

I like to think of margin-backed put selling in terms of speed limits. When you drive in a new car on an unfamiliar road with a sixty mile-per-hour speed limit, it's probably best to keep it at sixty. It's safe, and you'll never get a ticket. With time and experience on that road and a car you feel safe with, it's probably okay to take it up to sixty-five. On occasion, with particularly clear conditions and traffic moving along at seventy or better, you likely won't get a ticket at sixty-nine or seventy miles per hour. Go above that, and you incur undue safety risks and the possibility of a speeding ticket. Same thing with margin-backed put sales on DCs. With up to 5 percent of your account value, there's little risk. As you get more comfortable and better understand the risks and how to mitigate them, maybe 10 percent is fine. Much above that, and you're taking more risk than makes sense.

11

REMEMBER, IT'S ALL NEGOTIABLE

EVERYTHING IN A REAL ESTATE DEAL IS NEGOTIABLE. Sellers have an asking price, and there's nothing wrong with offering a lower price. It may be uncomfortable, particularly if you're dealing with a broker who tells you, "It's worth what the seller is asking." As you move down the line, everything else in a real estate deal seems less negotiable. Mortgage lenders have price sheets that seem like granite. There are all kinds of other fees in a real estate transaction, and they all look like they're set in stone. They may be, but perhaps not always. Mortgage rates may be negotiable depending on the loan-to-value ratio you propose. The rate may be negotiable based on the term of the loan or your credit rating. The easiest way to find out how negotiable individual components of the real estate transaction are is to test multiple sources. Apply with multiple mortgage brokers or originators. Never consider their first price as the best you can get. Always say, "But XYZ bank is offering a lower rate." You'll be able to sense when you're at rock bottom. Never take the first price.

> *The easiest way to find out how negotiable individual components of the real estate transaction are is to test multiple sources.*

Stock brokers are no different. If you're just starting out with limited capital, your negotiating ability is limited. But as your account grows, it will improve your negotiating position, and your leverage will increase. What can you negotiate? Everything—and your negotiating success will be a function of your aggressiveness, skill, and the value of your account. Because your account will eventually be very large, you need to start early. There will be rejections, and you need to learn from that.

What can you negotiate? First, there are your stock purchase and sale fees. These fees were once very high, but as things have become more efficient and competitive, they've declined a lot. In fact, as of this writing, Charles Schwab just announced zero fees for online stock and option trades. TD Ameritrade followed suit a couple of days later. Anything more than zero is too much! Every dollar you spend on transaction fees is a dollar less that you'll have to invest. Imagine how those dollars saved will grow into perpetuity!

Because you're trading options, you must understand the option transaction fees you're charged. They're too high unless they're zero! That's always the right answer. You can always get the lower fee somewhere else. It helps to know where the fees are lower. Publications like *Barron's* that do annual reviews of brokers and their fee structures are helpful in this regard. It's best to know those numbers when you meet with your broker.

Margin rates can be an important consideration, and they're negotiable too. Find out what others are offering before you meet with your broker. Your broker is used to folks simply paying the fees and rates they ask. You need to be different. You're essentially dealing with a used car retailer. If you agree to all the terms as stated, *mazel tov*. You'll be their favorite guy this week. But that's not your purpose. You want the best deal now.

The deal you have with your broker now is not forever. It's easy to become complacent. You've been paying those fees and rates for a long time, so what's to worry about? Lots! As your account and fees increase over time, your negotiating position also increases. The more income you generate for your broker, the less he wants to lose you and the more you want to threaten to leave. From the broker's standpoint, it's costly to acquire new clients. It's better for them to charge a couple bucks less in reduced fees and rates to retain an existing client like you.

Don't take this tug-of-war over fees and rates personally. If you don't, then your broker is less likely to do so. You simply want to be the most efficient investor you can be. If you can find a lower fee for a service someplace else, you need to tell your broker and ask her to match it. It never hurts to ask. You're competing against a vast universe of investors, and you need every advantage you can get. Plus, you have your investment strategy. You're not dependent on your broker for advisory services.

The rate of return on your cash balance is important too. Brokers usually sweep your cash into cash management accounts with very low rates of return. They may invest in higher returning instruments and pay you the lower rates. Hey, brokers have to make a living too. Let someone else pay for their living. You need to inquire about options. We sweep our available cash into the Vanguard Federal Money Market Fund Investor (VMFXX). The current return is about 2.2 percent, which is about 200 basis points (2 percent) higher than the brokers' standard cash management account. Two percent—that's a big difference! Managing the VMFXX requires a bit more time. We have to keep an eye on our available cash and buy more shares in VMFXX when cash accumulates. We have to sell VMFXX shares to meet the cash requirements as puts strike and to avoid incurring interest costs if the purchases are paid from our margin account. More active management of cash is a small price to pay for the additional return.

Never negotiate fees and rates with your broker by yourself. That's a strict rule of mine. You're investing for your family, and they should be there to understand the techniques you use to advance their future. In doing so, you educate future generations that everything is negotiable. Never pass up an opportunity to invite your children or grandchildren to meet with your broker when you plan to arm wrestle fees and rates. Not only do you achieve lower costs, but you train your family how to negotiate. You're negotiating to improve your heirs' position, but you're also training them about the importance of negotiating to improve their heirs' position.

In this world, there's no fixed price for anything. Everything is available in an auction. That could be a car or a suit or a movie ticket. Or it could be brokerage fees and margin rates. You should know the best rates and prices for everything you buy. That doesn't mean you necessarily buy at the lowest price. But it does mean you know the lowest price available, so you can negotiate the rates you want for the services you need. Teaching your heirs to negotiate and manage transaction fees is an integral feature of this succession planning system.

We've all heard the expression, "If you have to ask the price, you can't afford it." "It" can be anything. Remembering that expression might intimidate some folks. They don't like to think of themselves as cheapskates. Forget that. Price is always important. I always ask my children and grandchildren, "Who do you think first invented that expression? Was it a buyer or a seller?" It was obviously a seller who used it to shut down a buyer that was trying to negotiate price. Price is important.

If you like your broker and her firm and service, tell everyone about her. Then make sure she knows you do that. Name names and keep score on those who open accounts. The more referrals you have, the better your negotiating position.

12

INVESTING IN REAL ESTATE

THIS CHAPTER WILL BE SOMEWHAT SUBJECTIVE, as I draw on my own life experience regarding various forms of real estate investing. There are many different forms, but traditional real estate investing is as much about running a business as it is about investing. You need to be prepared for that, and that's a point we make several times. I share our experience and advice through some humorous—and sometimes painful—anecdotes that stress the personal intensity required for successful real estate investing.

There are many books about real estate investing that delve into the mathematics and tax consequences. I deal with the subject from a more strategic perspective. That is, how real estate might fit into a strategy for making your family rich and what the risks and challenges are.

Investing in real estate is often the most hyped opportunity to get rich quick. It's how I got started on making our family rich and is an area in which I continue to work. There are all kinds of TV shows about how to buy foreclosures and how to fix and flip homes. You may be invited to participate in seminars or meet-ups that focus on everything from investing in mortgages to tax certificate auctions. I've done it all and have mostly enjoyed the experiences, but sometimes only in hindsight. I've made money in virtually every aspect of real estate investing. But, at its core, most forms of real estate investing are complex, time intensive, and energy consuming because they are as much about operating a business as making and managing an investment. To be successful, you need a wide range of skills. Without them, there can be dangers.

> *...at its core, most forms of real estate investing are complex, time intensive, and energy consuming because they are as much about operating a business as making and managing an investment*

Real estate can be particularly appealing to a young investor who has limited funds. He or she can control a significant amount of capital with little paid-in equity because mortgage financing up to 80 or 90 percent of the property value may be readily available. That kind of leverage on residential rental real estate will generally pose less risk than similar leverage secured by stock, so real estate may be an enticing place to start for young, capital-strapped investors. It was for me many years ago.

There are also more passive ways to invest in real estate by investing in stocks or investing with private partnerships. We'll talk about those options at the end of this chapter, but this chapter is mainly about those one-off deals that involve most real estate practitioners.

Real estate is often a government-subsidized investment. The government wants to help you become a real estate investor. If it's the home you own and live in, you can deduct the interest and taxes you pay from your taxable income. When you sell, you can usually avoid any taxable gain. You can keep doing that throughout your life, constantly buying more expensive properties. Then, when you die, your home passes to your heirs, and they take it at the then current market value, thereby escaping capital gains taxes entirely. Of course, depending on the overall value of your estate, there could be estate taxes due.

If your real estate is investment property that you rent to others, then you can expense the depreciation each year. Depreciation is the presumed amount the value of the improvements will decrease each year. In many cases, the property value goes up, but you can still deduct the depreciation expense as though it were any other real, out-of-pocket expense. You can't depreciate the value of the underlying land because land is presumed not to deteriorate in value and not to diminish over time in the same way as improvements. So, in a way, the government also subsidizes your investment in rental real estate.

Depreciation is a great way to shelter other sources of income from income taxes. I've invested in real estate in a variety of ways all my adult life. Looking back, there's a lot I'd do differently, and maybe you can learn from my experience. The most important thing to emphasize, and we'll keep repeating this point, is that traditional real estate investing is not only an investment, it's also a business. As a business, it will often take a substantial amount of your time and energy. Let's look at various ways to invest in real estate and our experience with each.

Your Home

If there's a no-brainer in real estate investing, it may be the investment you make in your own home. Again, the government promotes home ownership by providing very favorable mortgage financing in the form of low interest rates and high leverage. Leverage is the amount of debt that can be applied in purchasing the property. A loan for 80 percent of the value of the property is said to have 80 percent leverage, or a loan-to-value (LTV) rate of 80 percent. In addition, the government allows homeowners to deduct the cost of interest on their mortgage as well as the real estate taxes paid. Recent changes to the tax code affect the amount and value of these deductions. You need to figure out the specifics for your situation based on your income. From an investment standpoint, the government makes it advantageous to own your own home. Circumstances will differ with location. For example, buying a home in a declining area may not work out so well. Your job situation may also impact the desirability of investing in a home. If you're vulnerable to frequent relocations, home ownership might not work well for you from an investment standpoint. Homes can be somewhat illiquid—they may be difficult to sell in particular areas and under certain market conditions. Transaction costs for buying and selling a home are high compared to other asset classes and can quickly wipe out any gain you may otherwise experience. We've bought and sold a number of personal residences over fifty years and have never lost money, but generally, we've owned in prosperous and growing areas. Markets like Detroit, Baltimore, Nevada, and Florida have had very severe busts where values can take decades to rebound.

Then there's the satisfaction you may feel in owning your own home. It's hard to quantify that factor, and it may be more important to you than the potential investment return and risks. You have to live somewhere, and if you feel that primal urge to own your own home, the government wants you to do so and makes it relatively easy to accomplish that goal. But remember, that home may tie you down, the investment may be difficult to sell, and transaction costs are high.

Rental Homes

We've also owned residential rental properties for over fifty years. After you own your own home, for some people the next logical next step is to invest in rental homes. This investment option is a whole lot like work, particularly if you manage your own property. No one likes to manage residential rentals. That includes real estate management companies that promote themselves as property management specialists. There are exceptions, but from my experience, not many. Outsourcing the management can be expensive, and the quality of the service is often spotty.

No one likes to manage residential rentals. That includes real estate management companies that promote themselves as property management specialists.

If you manage the property yourself, brace yourself for a constant stream of calls, texts, and emails complaining about everything from leaks to faulty appliances.

Alice

There was my rat lady; let's call her Alice. Alice worked for the CIA. Yep, that CIA. She was a single woman who lived in a small condo we've owned for years. She was a tenant for about seven years, and it was clear she relished her privacy. You'd expect that from a CIA employee, right? She paid annual rent increases, never complained, and was the perfect tenant in every way—at least until the day the condo association manager called. It seems the building engineer entered her condo while she was out to investigate the origin of a leak. What he found was a condo full of rats. Not the pet kind kept in cages, but free-range guys. It later became clear that Alice also had become a hoarder who bought endless amounts of stuff on TV and stacked all that stuff in the small condo, conveniently providing living and breeding quarters for the rats. Rats are apparently difficult to potty train, and Alice fed them dog food, bypassing niceties like bowls. So, all over the place, there was lots of . . . well, you get the picture.

What to do? The condo is in northern Virginia, and I lived in Florida at the time. I called Alice, thinking it really couldn't be that bad. It turns out Alice was having a bit of a tough emotional time, and the only comfort she had was from her rat friends. She started with a couple, and over time—apparently a rather long time—nature took its course. Alice recognized that we now had a problem with the condo association because rats were not among authorized pets, nor were they approved as service animals, no matter the comfort Alice drew from them in her time of distress. Alice struggled a bit trying to understand why folks might be upset with all her free-range rats, but she did acknowledge their presence violated the rules.

Alice apparently had a brother living in Europe and an elderly dad in Chicago. Let's call her dad Mike. By the time I called Mike, he was aware of the problem and prepared to drive to Virginia to check on his daughter.

Meanwhile, back at the condo, the mostly elderly female residents had found out about the free-range rats. They wanted action, for fear that Alice's friends' range would widen to include their units. With Dad heading to town and the landlord coming from Florida, from the residents' perspective, the condo association was too slow to take action. What to do? How about calling the fire department to report smoke? Was there smoke? A minor detail. So, the fire department arrived, complete with axes, the jaws of life, and all their other equipment. Although the building manager had provided them a key, that was all too slow, so they took the heavy metal entry door down. What good is all that equipment if you don't use it? Fortunately, the rats didn't come out. The critters were apparently reluctant to leave the comfort of home and those randomly disbursed piles of dog food. But no smoke and no fire—crafty old ladies, those.

Dad showed up first and expressed his shock at the condition of the condo and Alice's state of mind. He quickly got Alice medical help. Mike assured me he'd take care of everything. Not to worry. With Mike's assurance, I arranged for a remediation firm to come in and give an estimate for the work. Those are the firms that have guys in space suits with masks for decontaminating toxic areas. This is not cheap. After Mike admitted his daughter to the hospital, he had the remediation firm remove Alice's belongings and put whatever was salvageable in storage. Mike paid for that work, and it ended there for him.

Mike was getting a bit long in the tooth, and maybe he forgot those promises he made. All the rest of the work, including the decontamination, still remained to be completed. Everything needed to be bagged and removed to a special dump, all by guys in space suits. Carpets had to be bagged and sent for incineration, and the concrete floors had to be specially treated to deal with the rats' waste.

It seems the little darlings like to gnaw on wood, so all the baseboards, moldings, and interior doors had to be replaced. All the cabinetry in the kitchen and bathroom had to be removed. All appliances were contaminated and had to go. In all, there was about an additional $15,000 that I had to cover, and neither Mike nor Alice answered my calls.

In the end, I took the opportunity to fully renovate the unit and re-rent it at a higher rate. Sure, we could have sued, but Alice was either crazy or in delicate health, and Mike had no legal liability. So, take the lemons and make lemonade, so to speak.

Think this is a unique experience? Not so fast—eventually Alice was released from the hospital and is now someone else's tenant. No one called me for a reference.

The Parkers

You might get a kick out of this next experience. I was temporarily working in California, and I got a call from a favorite realtor to tell me she had a terrific opportunity in my neighborhood in northern Virginia. In fact, the home she had to sell was similar to mine and constructed by the same builder. The story was that the elderly owners, let's call them Mr. and Mrs. Parker, wanted to do a sale leaseback. It appeared their principal asset was their home, and they wanted to take out some money to travel freely in their golden years. Mrs. Parker worked for the British Embassy, and Mr. Parker was an employee of the Washington, D.C. government. The realtor was a Brit who tossed in the fact that Mrs. Parker was Winston Churchill's secretary during World War II. The sales price and rent were right, so what's not to like?

I called my investing partner back in Virginia, and he loved the deal as much as I did. We put together an offer, and the Parkers promptly accepted it. We documented the deal, arranged financing, and scheduled a closing. Tom, the partner, attended the settlement, after which I got a call. He said, "Pat, the way you pitched this deal, I thought we were dealing with Ma and Pa Kettle. The people who showed up for settlement were more like Bonnie and Clyde." I'll never forget that line. Tom went on to tell me that the Parkers received no proceeds from closing. Everything went to settle liens and judgments. So, Tom smelled a rat. (Sorry to mix stories!)

The Parkers paid rent for a couple of months and everything was fine, and then it wasn't. After about five months, the rent stopped. We went through the notices and threats and eventually took legal action for eviction and damages. This is where it really gets good. The Parkers countersued us for radon poisoning. It turns out they got a radon inspector to write a letter attesting to high levels of radon in the basement, which caused all manner of maladies for the aging Parkers, poor dears. Did we mention that the Parkers had owned and lived in the house for fifteen years prior to the sale?

A hearing followed, and the judge found for the landlord. Then the Parkers appealed, and the judge required that they post a bond. Suspecting now that they had no assets, we asked ourselves how they would post a bond. Silly us. Turns out the Parkers got a bank letter of credit from a local community bank—the same bank where we were clients and also owned stock. When we called our buddy at the bank, it became clear that the Parkers owed the bank a significant amount and threatened to default if the bank didn't post the letter of credit. In the end, the Parkers lost on appeal, but it took another couple of months of no rent.

One day, the sheriff and a moving truck showed up, and the Parkers moved out. As I stood on the home's steps, a UPS truck pulled up and delivered a pair of custom-made British men's shoes with an invoice for $800. At the time, I doubt I'd ever spent more than $100 for shoes.

We received the proceeds from the letter of credit, which paid our lawyer. The British embassy informed us they wouldn't enforce a judgment against an employee, and Mr. Parker quit his job with the D.C. government. We did collect a few other dollars. The Parkers annually hosted an American-Brit Fourth of July party on the top floor of a local hotel. They had to post a deposit for the reservation. We garnished and collected that deposit, and I always wondered if they went ahead with the party.

Colonel White

Back in the early 1980s, I lived in Fairfax County, Virginia, where I bought houses, furnished them, and rented them to tenants at premium rates for short terms, mostly to families waiting for a house to be built. Builders were happy to have a place to park their buyers until their homes were completed.

That worked great for a while, and then things cooled off as they always do. One of the houses had been vacant for a month or two when along came Colonel White. He said he was a former Air Force pilot who'd moved from Colorado where he'd been injured in an aircraft accident. He needed to be in the D.C. area to have access to the military medical institutions and the Pentagon while he worked out the details of a disability retirement. He drove a new

Cadillac and said he needed to have a house with a garage. His family would follow as soon as they sold their place in Colorado. The Colonel said he hadn't had time to open a bank account and wanted to pay two months' rent up front, and the two months' security deposit seemed reasonable to him. Four months' up front in cash! Did I mention we'd been vacant for a spell?

I jumped at the deal and signed him up. I owned a couple of other furnished homes in the area and had only one lawn mower for all the units. It came as no surprise that Colonel White arranged for the daughter of another tenant, who was also a colonel, to mow his lawn. When I was in the neighborhood, it struck me as strange that the Cadillac was always parked in the driveway. Months passed, and the Colonel was always on time with the rent in cash.

One Saturday morning, on the front page of the *Washington Post*, the headline announced the largest drug bust in Fairfax County history, and there with his hands locked around the back of his neck was none other than the good Colonel. It seems Colonel White was not in the military. He was an escaped convict from a federal prison in Washington state. He was flying to Mexico and bringing back drugs that he processed in my house. What did he use to pay for the drugs? The counterfeit bills he printed in the garage.

It gets better. The raid on the house was a coordinated effort by Fairfax County police, the Secret Service (because of the counterfeiting), the Drug Enforcement Administration, and the FBI (escaped con). Apparently, they were all in the area in various commercial vehicles when someone blew a whistle and the assault began, complete with battering rams applied to my various doors. There's just something about first responders and doors.

It gets better yet. The raid took place while Colonel Number Two's fourteen-year-old daughter was mowing Colonel White's lawn. When I got to the house that Sunday morning, the police were still everywhere. There were dogs, and the cops were digging up the yard looking for drugs. Oh, and there was a very honked off Colonel Number Two. The place was a complete mess.

Among the assembled crowd was a nineteen-year-old Filipino girl, her parents, and a couple of younger brothers. The young lady was the girlfriend of the fiftyish Colonel White. It quickly became apparent in conversation with the girl that she'd been released by the police. The only unencumbered asset owned by Colonel White was the three months' rent I then held. Apparently, the Colonel and his companion were strapped for cash, and she quickly inquired about what she could do to get the money refunded. Fortunately, her dad was a skilled carpenter, and we agreed on the things that he could do to get any recovery. A week or so later, he'd finished the tasks, and I refunded about $4,000 after I'd visited the Colonel in the pokey to secure a written release and his apology. He still seemed like a nice guy, albeit a lying, drug-dealing, counterfeiting, military-impersonating jailbird. For a couple of years afterward, police still showed up occasionally with dogs to sniff out the yard for buried drugs. Kind of spiced up the relations with future tenants.

A week or so later, the *Washington Post* announced the arrest of the young woman for an attempt to bribe a Fairfax County Corrections Officer with $4,000 for the release of the good colonel. Love knows no bounds.

I've rented to hundreds of tenants. Most of the time, everything works fine. In these stories, you could argue that I could have avoided the problems with better due diligence, but I've had plenty of other problems where I did full due diligence.

Technically, I made money on these deals and virtually all of my other residential real estate investments. But how do you measure profit? Is it simply the difference between buying and selling prices? How do you factor in the enormous amount of time and work involved in resolving all the problems associated with owning and managing real estate?

The above stories are extreme examples of problems with residential rental real estate. It's one of the easiest investment vehicles for small investors to get involved in. It might be right for you, but you must understand that after you start down the path of investing in real estate, you're running a business. It's a way for most people to make money over time, but I think there are more efficient, easier ways to make your family rich.

One final suggestion. If you're seriously considering getting involved with residential rental real estate, see the movie *Pacific Heights* first. You think my stories are scary!

Real Estate Lending

Another way to invest in real estate is by originating mortgages to owners, secured by their real estate. The standard mortgage markets are very efficient, so borrowers with good credit who borrow against solid value in their homes or investment properties have little trouble getting mortgage loans at reasonable rates. For the most part, it makes no sense to try to compete with the national mortgage brokers or local banks to originate loans. That's where "hair" comes in. Mortgage lending, like traditional real estate lending, is as much about operating a business as investing. In fact, it may be more so. So, the only mortgage investing that warrants the amount of time required are deals with hair, or complications.

> *...the only mortgage investing that warrants the amount of time required are deals with hair, or complications.*

For some years, we operated a hard money lending business. That means we lent to investors at very high rates for projects that would be hard to fund from conventional sources. The truth is, hard money lenders like us are, in a real sense, lending to the property rather than the borrower. A hard money loan is predicated on the idea that the lender will eventually have to take the property in a foreclosure and will only get his money back by reselling the property, which is the security for the loan. We typically charge a 15 percent annual interest rate and a 5 percent origination fee for a three- to five-year loan. That means the unamortized balance of the loan is due in three to five years—that, at a time when a homeowner could borrow for thirty years at about a 5 percent fixed rate with a half point origination fee. That's a big difference, and the difference is all about hair.

In the typical hard money loan, the borrower may be inexperienced or has had prior credit problems. The property may be in a sketchy area or in poor condition. For example, we've lent for years to a West African developer who buys large townhouses in developing areas of Washington, D.C. and converts them to four-unit condominiums. Such a project, though relatively small, is complex, risky, and a ton of work. Rather than be the developer who invests in the property and renovates and markets the units, we can just sit back and make the loan, right? The returns are good, and the work is limited when things work well. But they never work well. There are always complications and delays. That can be a good thing from one standpoint, because the typical hard money deal has lots of high-cost penalties. But deals can only sustain so many costs and penalties before a borrower balks and walks, and voila, you, the lender, are a real estate investor in an unfinished four-unit condo conversion in the ghetto.

It's always worked out for us. Either the deal works mostly as planned, and we collect our fees and interest and move on to the next deal with a borrower who's now a bit less of a default risk, or we take the property in a foreclosure—or what's called a deed in lieu—and arrange one kind of workout or another. Deed in lieu is a term that describes a situation in which the borrower is in such bad shape that he agrees to give the lender a deed in lieu of going through the fore-closure process. We've done that too, and it's always worked out. But it takes time, knowledge, financial endurance, and persistence. And what does all that add up to? A business! So, if you become a mortgage lender, it's mostly like becoming a traditional real estate investor. You're an investor, but you're also operating a business.

We've found that if you operate a real estate investing business, you inevitably get involved in lending. One way or the other, you'll become a lender. It may be you sell a property, and the buyer has some issues and you need to take back some financing to make the sale, or one of your contractors goes into the fix-and-flip business and you help him out by financing his acquisitions. When you understand the real estate investing business, you tend to expand from owning to lending, or you migrate into other areas like buying foreclosures or tax certificate investing.

Foreclosures

Buying foreclosures is about getting captured by the bargain bug. You want to be a traditional real estate investor, but you believe it's all about buying *right*, and how can it get better than to buy property at foreclosures? Foreclosures come to market because the owner has been unable to meet his financial obligations to his lender, and the lender forecloses or forces a sale of the property to satisfy the unpaid loan. There are many books about the laws of foreclosure and how to get great deals through foreclosure sales, and this isn't the place to repeat all that. Let's just say the principles are simple, but the law and practice can be very complex. It's a great way to get good deals, but the risks are high, and you need to be well-versed in the law of foreclosure. Even then, you'll need to be intimately involved in all aspects of the process. Foreclosure sales are about real estate investing, but it requires the kind of time and attention involved in running a business.

Some years ago, I saw a foreclosure notice (lenders usually must advertise a foreclosure in a local paper) for a valuable parcel of land in a desirable community in northern Virginia. Foreclosures are typically conducted by an auctioneer or attorney on the local courthouse steps. To be eligible to bid, you need a certified check or bank check accepted in advance by the auctioneer that qualifies you to bid. In this case, the bidders needed a $10,000 certified check. I got the check from the bank that morning and showed up on the courthouse steps, only to discover the borrower had brought the loan current and the lender had withdrawn the foreclosure action. That happens frequently, and you just chalk it up to the nature of the business. As I turned on my heels to head back to the bank to redeposit the check, the attorney called another sale in a local condominium complex I knew. I already had the check burning a hole in my pocket, so why not take a shot at the property?

In the typical foreclosure, the lender who brings the action opens the process by bidding the amount necessary to satisfy his loan. If no one else bids, the lender buys the property and then strives to resell it on the market to capture all or as much as he can of the amount owed to him. That's what happened here. The lender bid his balance, which seemed to me a relatively low number. Now mind you, I had no idea of the size of the unit. It could be an efficiency or a one-, two-, or three-bedroom unit. The value would vary markedly depending on the size. I had the check, and I knew and liked the complex. After the lender opened the bidding, he dropped out, and there was only one other bidder: he and I, mano a mano, back and forth, until I finally outbid the other fellow. It was mine! That's the good news.

The bad news was that the lender's attorney, as the guy bidding on behalf of the mortgagee (lender), promptly notified me I had fifteen days to close the transaction, no exceptions. It's very difficult to arrange a mortgage loan in fifteen days. It's infinitely more difficult to arrange a mortgage on a foreclosure property in fifteen days. The attorney told me to come up with the balance in cash pronto, or he'd foreclose again, and hasta la vista to my $10,000. That's right, my $10,000 was at risk, and I could lose it if I didn't close. He was not a nice, patient fellow.

What follows is not kosher, and you shouldn't do it if you make foreclosures your business. But if you do invest in foreclosures, you'll likely do a lot of edgy things. I had no idea what I'd bought other than the unit number, and before I ponied up the balance, I had to find out whether it made any sense to close at the purchase price I'd bid. It might make more sense to walk away from the $10,000, or perhaps whine about it and try to get the lender to have mercy and refund the deposit.

I know this guy Sal, who's a locksmith. If you're in real estate, you get to know a lot of guys. The next day, Sal and I went to the unit, and Sal plied his trade. There's no polite way to say this: Sal picked the lock. But the door wouldn't open. The interior chain was on. Someone lived in the unit, and that someone promptly appeared in the form of Clarence, as I would soon learn. Through the crack in the door I could see Clarence, clothed at midday in pajamas held together by clothes pins. Now there's a scene. Yours truly, this get-rich-quick foreclosure investor with his lock-picking cohort and the elderly—and apparently infirm—owner and foreclosuree. Did I mention this foreclosure business can be complex?

It turns out that Clarence was recovering from a recent medical procedure and suffered from post-operative depression. In his depressed state, he apparently failed to pay his bills, including his mortgage and condo fees. I would later find out that Clarence had plenty of money but had simply stopped functioning due to the depression. We began a series of negotiations. I started to bring food and passed it through the chained door. Clarence was embarrassed by his situation and refused to let me in, but he did tell me his unit

was an efficiency. Considering the price I'd paid, Clarence had employed a fairly effective marketing approach to selling his unit.

Time was running out, and I discovered the local county government had a senior intervention specialist. One day, I told Clarence that he and I were in a bad spot. I was about to lose $10,000
and he was going to be foreclosed again. I asked him if he'd let the
county social worker in to discuss his lifestyle options. He consent-
ed after I plied him with particularly tasty home-baked raisin bran
muffins. While I sat in the lobby, he and the social worker talked.
They showed up a couple of hours later with some bags, and off
Clarence went to a nursing home. End of story? Not hardly.

I still hadn't closed, but the owner was finally gone. My only
right and obligation was to close, and all of this drama should have
taken place afterward. I closed for cash, unable to secure a mortgage
in the time available.

After I took possession, I needed to take care of Clarence's
stuff. The condo, though small, was chock full of Clarence's belongings. In the middle of the unit sat one of those electric reclin-
ers. The electric part didn't work, but the chair served as Clarence's
filing cabinet. On it was a stack of documents that started at the
bottom with the settlement sheet for the condo from years earlier.
Like the rings of a tree, the pile showed the progression of Clarence's life as a homeowner. Each year, he received a single Christ-
mas card from his sister in upstate New York. Every card said the
same thing: "Bud (his nick name), we'd love to hear from you."
I called her, and her initial question was, "How is Bud?" When
I told her he'd gone into a nursing home, she asked only if he'd
done so voluntarily.

It turns out, Clarence was retired and received a nice pension.
He had plenty of money in his account. He also had a ten-year-old
car with 4,000 miles on it. The court appointed a trustee and sold
his stuff.

Clarence was a shy guy, but he prospered in the retirement home setting. Over time, he got progressively stronger. Soon, he moved up to more independent living. Clarence smoked, and he drank bourbon, and I dropped by periodically with a couple of packs of cigarettes and a bottle of bourbon. There came a time when he moved into a school building that had been converted to small living units with a monitor at the end of each hall. One day, I stopped by with the smokes and booze and went to his unit. No Clarence. The monitor told me Clarence was probably in the smoking room at the end of the corridor.

Remember that, up until this time, Clarence didn't know anyone locally. Usually when I showed up with his smokes and booze, Clarence was so glad to see me that if he'd had a tail, he would have wagged it violently. This particular day, when I showed up at the entrance to the smoking room, I saw Clarence on a couch with an elderly lady whose dress was hiked up to her waist. Seeing me, he instantly looked at his watch as if to say, "Let's make this quick, Pat." He rose, accepted the cigarettes and the bourbon, and hustled me on my way. That was the last time I saw Clarence. My foreclosure was complete when I knew he was in good hands, so to speak.

I have lots of foreclosure stories. We've always made money, but you get the picture. While one-off real estate investing can be satisfying and lucrative, it's complicated, risky, and labor intensive. Whether it's buying, mortgage lending, managing, fixing and flipping, or foreclosures, you'll be running a business. It may be full time or part time, but it's a business. You have to expect to be intensely involved, not only to make money but to also protect your capital.

Tax Certificates

I'd like to mention another form of real estate investing, which is buying tax certificates. The practice varies from state to state, but it's much like buying foreclosures. Tax certificates come up for investment when a real estate owner has failed to pay his real estate taxes. Then, the local taxing authority auctions off certificates. In effect, the buyer of the certificate pays the taxes due and earns the right to receive payment plus interest from the property owner.

Tax certificates come up for investment when a real estate owner has failed to pay his real estate taxes.

Tax certificate investing can be a lucrative opportunity if you pick the right properties. The property owner will almost always pay off the certificate rather than lose the property. Jurisdictions use a variety of methods to give the tax certificate owner the right to take ownership of the property over time if the original owner hasn't paid off the certificate owner plus interest. Investing in tax certificates can be complex and fraught with risks.

If the owner doesn't redeem the property on which you bought a certificate, you typically acquire the right to take ownership of the property after a number of years. Typically, depending on the jurisdiction, you must request a tax deed that transfers the title of the property to the holder of the tax certificate. It's rare that a tax certificate holder acquires a very valuable property in a tax certificate sale. The owner usually has plenty of time to arrange financing or a sale to pay off the certificate. But if you pick the right properties to bid on, you can earn nice returns, often in the 12 to 15 percent annual range. On occasion, you may also acquire a property at a very nice price.

Community Banks

Investing in community banks is my favorite form of real estate investing. Whether you engage in all the various forms of real estate investing or specialize in one form, you'll need reliable banking relationships. Note, that's plural: relationships. When you deal with local banks, it's important to understand that everything is negotiable, and your best negotiating tool is to have more than one source of financing. That's a good lesson in all forms of investing. Your options are only as good as your second source of funding. You'll get the best terms only if your banker understands that you have another source. So, from the outset of your real estate investing, curry more than one banking relationship.

We've always preferred community banks that are located in the areas in which we work. Large national banks typically are too bureaucratic and difficult to create the kind of relationship you'll need to accomplish your deals. You also want to work with public community banks—banks in which you can buy and own stock.

> *As a rough rule of thumb, we never deal with a local bank in which we don't own stock.*

As a rough rule of thumb, we never deal with a local bank in which we don't own stock.

In some ways, our bank stock investments have been our most successful real estate investments. Looking back, our bank investments have typically paid a dividend. Further, for years now, larger community banks have often bought our small banks. When that happens, we typically receive a pop in value of about 30 percent.

None of the banks we owned ten years ago still exist today in their original form. Every one of them has been acquired, and we received either cash or stock in the acquiring bank. We've invested in community banks for forty years or more and have never lost money, and in most cases, we've realized significant long-term returns. The truth is, investing in community banks requires a whole lot less effort and, in many ways, is much more satisfying than the various forms of active real estate investing. We all know that banks have had significant difficulties over time. Like all businesses, including real estate, banks can be cyclical. But remember, you're in this for the long term. You plan to make your family rich, and they're forever.

Depending on the size of your local community banks, their stock may be somewhat illiquid. There may not be a lot of float or stock available to purchase at any given time. In some cases, stock sales may even be private, and you may have to arrange a purchase through the bank president or other senior bank official. Most community banks trade publicly, but may trade only a couple of hundred or a few thousand shares daily. The less float and liquidity of a particular bank stock, the more it will affect the bid and ask prices. Briskly traded stocks often have only a penny or a few cents difference between bid and ask prices. It's not uncommon for bid and ask spreads on more thinly traded stocks to vary by as much as a dollar or more, so you must be careful in your buying practices. It usually helps to place your bid below the current bid and leave it outstanding for the day.

There are a couple of other things you need to keep in mind when you invest in community banks, particularly if you intend your bank investing to advance your real estate investment business. We employ the following practices:

- **Never use the drive-thru window**. If you buy an interest in a bank, that bank is your business. You want to take every opportunity to know the people and let them get to know you. You'll learn nothing about your business through a drive-up window. Think of it like a restaurant. You don't learn much about a restaurant by ordering at the drive-thru. If you owned a restaurant and wanted to know how things were going, you'd go in and sit down, right? The same works for banks. Go into the branch to handle your business. When you deal with a teller or anyone else, start off with, "How's business?" You care, because it's your business. It's also good to know if the bank employees own the stock. How do you find that out? You ask. I often say something like, "The stock was up nicely last month. Did you see that?" When they answer, I might ask, "Do you own the stock?" It tells me a lot if the employees broadly own the stock. Then I know I'm dealing not only with a bank employee, but a fellow owner—my business partner. You can't learn all that through a drive-thru lane.

- **Always attend the annual meeting**. Every publicly-owned community bank has an annual meeting. It's mostly a formality, and very few stockholders other than the insiders attend. But there are a lot of good reasons you should always attend. First, they usually feed you, and the food, in my experience, is typically good. If the meeting is in the afternoon, there will often be an open bar. In the case of smaller community banks, it's common for only twenty or so stockholders to attend. That's a good thing because the ones who are there have a better chance to make their presence known. The chief lending officer will always be there, and that's the person you want to make your best friend. You want him or her to know you're there and that you're a shareholder. Do that, and I guarantee the next time you apply for a loan, you'll get better treatment. The last thing the bank wants is a dissatisfied customer who's also a shareholder to show up at an annual meeting.

    The senior bank officers typically make a formal presentation that summarizes the bank's performance. By the time of the annual meeting, which usually takes place in the spring, the bank will have issued its annual report for the prior calendar year. With experience, you'll pick up on the nuances in the presentation, discussion, and questions. You'll hear any recurring patterns of problems and what the bank plans to do about them. You also want to know if it's mostly good news and a seemingly rosy future.

Over time, you'll get a feel for where the bank is going. Is there a positive culture of success, or do problems seem to keep popping up? Problems may not be an entirely bad thing. That's because an underperforming bank may be vulnerable to a buyout, and those almost always involve a premium price over the current market.

A couple of years ago, we experienced a number of takeovers in the community banks we owned, and I was looking around for a new community bank with which to initiate a relationship. A new relationship for us always involves buying the stock. I found a bank that had rapid growth and paid a nice increasing dividend. This particular bank, despite its rapid growth, clearly controlled its expenses. We bought a couple hundred shares, and I resolved to keep a close eye on their progress. That included going to the annual meeting.

I thought that everything looked good, and I continued to buy small amounts of the stock. The president of the bank was a young woman, which is uncommon in banking in that area. In fact, she was the only female community bank CEO in the region and also one of the youngest CEOs. The fact that she was female didn't matter to me, but her age did. That's because, in my experience, a bank is less likely to sell out when the leadership is young. Older executives tend to be more likely to want to cash out and rest on their laurels—not always, but often when compared to younger leaders—and I like to have the 30 percent or so pop sooner rather than later.

By the time I attended the second annual meeting, I'd only heard good news. The bank continued to open new branches without impairing its profitability. In recent years, many banks—including community banks—had opted for fewer branches in favor of more reliance on technology. I'd heard community bank officials remark that fewer customers came into their branches and preferred, instead, to use technology-based transactions. But this bank kept expanding its footprint in the metropolitan area with little appreciable negative impact on profitability. Did I mention that each year they also increased the dividend?

At the second annual meeting I attended, a couple of interesting things happened. A local bank analyst for a regional brokerage firm was also there. This guy is frequently quoted on community banking matters in the local business pages. I'd known him casually and had seen him at other community bank annual meetings over the years. At this meeting, he got up and said to the president after her presentation, "You've done so well consistently over the years, I would have expected you by now to be teaching how to succeed in community banking." I'd never heard that before, particularly from a long-time local authority on community banking.

In the gathering that followed, I chatted with him, and he confirmed all my positive findings. I then spoke with the manager of a local fund that specialized in community bank investing. He also had a positive reaction to the bank's performance and confirmed that his fund continued to accumulate the bank's stock. How do you get better data than this?

After that meeting, I accelerated my accumulation of the stock and expanded my banking relationship. Before the next annual meeting, the bank announced a merger with another regional bank at a 35 percent premium in the stock price. As it happens, the acquiring bank was also an investment of mine that paid a very nice dividend. When I traded in my stock in the target bank for the acquiring bank's stock, my total holdings were significant, and they now represent my second largest community bank investment.

Can you imagine how pleased I was to attend those annual meetings? Even though so few folks attend, they always seem to be the right ones. A year after the buyout, I received an announcement that my favorite female former community bank CEO had quit the board of the acquiring bank. What was she planning to do? Start a de novo bank! I couldn't write the check fast enough to buy into the new bank.

- **Always attend the earnings calls**. When a community bank reaches about $2 billion in assets, they generally schedule regular earnings calls. Publicly-owned community banks issue quarterly reports on their performance, usually published a month or so after the close of the quarter. After a bank achieves a certain size, and that varies with each bank, they typically conduct a quarterly conference call in which the president and the chief financial officer present the results of the previous quarter. A series of questions, mostly from analysts who monitor the bank, immediately follows their presentation. Depending on the size of the bank, there may be several community bank analysts who focus on this particular institution. These are usually very smart folks immersed in the details of the bank who don't have the time to travel to annual meetings but do call in to the quarterly reports. Any stockholder can attend the earnings conference call. Anyone can ask questions, but usually only the analysts do so. You'll quickly realize that the bank's management knows all the analysts who follow their institution. Just as with annual meetings, you'll learn a lot from the quarterly earnings calls, and they usually last less than an hour.

- **Make a point to know and visit your loan officer(s)**. If you're a real estate investor, the single most important reason for being involved with your community bank is access to loans, and the single most important person in the bank is the head loan officer. You need to get to know him or her. It helps to find occasions to interact, even if that means you pop in to say hello when you visit the branch. Think of the loan officers as your partners. If you have investment partners, you talk with them regularly, not only when you need something. Do that with your loan officer too. Let him or her know what you're thinking, how your deals are performing, and what you see on the horizon. It doesn't hurt to find a way to let them know you talk with other lenders too.

- **Maintain a regular Personal Financial Statement (PFS).** If you have a loan with your local bank, they usually want a PFS at least every year. We update ours every month, but every quarter is probably often enough. Don't wait for the bank to ask. Forward an updated PFS to your lender(s) every year. Also, as soon as you file your annual tax return, send a copy to your loan officer. Your PFS should be in the form of a balance sheet that includes all your assets with footnotes that list all the details, including addresses, when acquired, purchase price, individual owners, and their interest in the asset. The footnotes can also include a synopsis of rentals and property management facts. The balance sheet also needs a very detailed list of all liabilities. The footnotes should contain all the data, including loan numbers, lenders' addresses, and contact information. An example of a PFS follows this chapter.

- Your tax return provides the best income statement, but you may need to maintain an Income Explanation Supplement to your tax return to communicate factors not obvious from your income tax return. For example, many real estate investors have relatively low taxable incomes because of all the depreciation expenses they claim. Depreciation is not a true cash cost and doesn't adversely affect your cash flow, but it does artificially suppress what appears to be your income.

Regularly maintaining a PFS will save you time and work in the end. It's a big effort to generate a PFS from scratch, but it's a piece of cake to do a routine monthly update.

- **Real Estate Investing: Some Guiding Principles** After fifty years of all kinds of real estate investing, here's what I've learned. These are the guiding principles I think are important for successful and satisfying investing:

  1. It's a Business. We can't say this enough. Real estate investing in its many forms is complex and usually personally intensive. By that, I mean it's hands on. Whether you outsource the management or do it yourself, you'll be personally involved. Real estate management is the one aspect of real estate investing that almost no one wants to do. Every aspect of real estate is more interesting than management. Consequently, it's always a challenge, no matter the market, to find smart, motivated, professional managers. It's simply a delusion to believe a manager cares as much about your property as you do. Inevitably, that means the investor must be involved and engaged.

  2. Location, Location, Location. That's what you always hear about real estate. But what does it mean? I think the best explanation I heard was from a young woman who spoke at a real estate investing meetup I attended some years ago in Austin, Texas. She explained that her family members were multigenerational real estate investors in the central Texas area that radiated out from the city of Austin. The speaker said, "My great-grandparents invested in central Texas real estate, but they wanted their investments to cash flow right away, and they didn't die rich." She continued, "My grandparents invested in the same area and also focused on cash flow, and they didn't die rich." Then she outlined her mother's investment strategy, which focused on a limited number of zip codes in the central Austin urban area. Austin has become a particularly prosperous metropolitan area that serves as the state's capital, an advanced learning center, as well as home to vibrant medical and technology industries. She concluded, "My mom will die very rich."

There's a lot of undeveloped land in Texas. Development can always expand farther away from urban cores to access less expensive land. Austin has challenging transportation issues and limited affordable housing options.

Here's what the speaker was saying. Her mother was willing to sacrifice immediate return for the longer-term yields available by focusing on areas of limited supply. There's a lot of land in Texas, a good deal of it undeveloped. Rising rents provide an incentive for developers and investors to go farther out from the center of the metropolitan area, but those properties in outlying areas don't appreciate as predictably as properties in the central urban core. As a metropolitan area grows, the relative value of the centrally located properties increases at a faster, more predictable rate. Those areas are much harder to duplicate. That's the scarcity value premium. But it's not always true. In certain metro areas, crime and blight may be so prevalent in the inner city that values stagnate and even decline over time.

It might help to think of the location aspect of real estate in terms of bonds. We all know that the higher the quality of the borrower, the lower the return on the bonds. The credit quality of the borrower or the security for the bonds helps determine the cost of the debt. In real estate, we speak of the return in terms of capitalization, or cap rate. The cap rate is simply the property's net income divided by the property value. Generally, the higher the cap rate, the lower the quality of the real estate investment. Real estate in better locations will typically command a lower cap rate.

There's a similar pattern in commercial real estate that results from the credit quality of the tenant and the duration of the lease. Generally, the higher the quality of the tenant and the longer the lease, the lower the cap rate. The more the lease contract obligation is like a longer-term bond, the more the property will be valued like a comparable term bond on the tenant.

3. Keep the Leverage in Bounds. One of the truly nice things about real estate is *leverage*. I think that's one of the reasons real estate investing attracts so many young people. They have limited capital, and real estate allows them to control significant capital with little money. For the most part, it's reasonably safe to keep debt on your property. Each month, your tenant's rent pays down the debt. It's just a Steady Eddie way to make money over time.

In an appreciating market, the debt amplifies your return. The math is pretty simple. If you bought a property for $100,000, and it goes up 5 percent in value, your return is roughly 5 percent. If you have a 50 percent mortgage on the property, and it goes up the same 5 percent, then your return is about 10 percent. Add to that 10 percent the amount you paid down on the principal amount of the loan, and your return goes up further. Then add the value of the depreciation expenses to offset income from other sources on your income taxes, and the return goes up even more.

But don't go crazy on debt. You'll have unforeseen operating expenses, and vacancies are likely. And then there are those down markets. I generally like to run each property almost as an independent business or profit center and keep my debt on each property at 70 percent or less of the purchase price.

4. Management's the Key. Many folks like to invest in real estate, but no one likes to manage it. Some years ago, I mentioned to my long-term partner that we'd be a whole lot richer if we'd simply kept all our real estate. Then I asked, "Why did we sell?" He responded, "Because Marilyn (his wife) quit." For a long time, Marilyn managed all our properties. Then, as the family responsibilities grew and the property management frustrations accumulated, Marilyn served notice that she no longer wanted the management duties. Neither my partner nor I had the time or appetite for management. After a couple of futile attempts to hire a replacement, we started to unload properties.

Later, we grew our real estate holdings with partners who agreed to manage the properties for a fee. These partners were generally short on cash, and we lent them the money necessary to buy their interest. That way, a cash-strapped young person could start to accumulate real estate equity and earn some income managing the properties.

It's very difficult to find a real estate manager who will manage your property as if it's their own. Unless they do own it. That's why partner-managers generally work for us. Our interests are congruent. One of our core principles is that we can make a bad deal work with the right partner, but we can't make a good deal work with the wrong partner. That's how important the quality of the partner is. They must be hard-working and trustworthy and, if possible, they need to have real equity in the deal.

5. Partnering. I've had partners in real estate deals for years. My experience had been that I could make a bad deal work with the right partner but couldn't make a good deal work with the wrong partner. In recent years, I've had some second thoughts. The reasons are many, but it's mainly because my partners and I differ on how to handle our assets.

My partners handle the property management our assets require, and, as discussed above, that's a key ingredient to successful real estate investing. They're great at managing our real estate and controlling the operating expenses, but there's another kind of management in real estate. That's asset management. An asset manager constantly monitors the investment in terms of how best to add value.

Suppose you and your partner invested in downtown surface parking lots. Income is pretty good, and your partner manages the operation for a reasonable fee. Your parking lot is in the path of downtown development and, over time, your property has a higher value for office building or multifamily development. But your partner is content with the revenue your parking lot generates, and they have neither the skills nor the instincts to be an office building or multifamily developer. You may be stuck in a partnership and a property use that made sense as an interim solution, but in a changing market, the income generated from your parking lot application doesn't keep pace with the market value of your property based on a higher and better use.

I know people have worse problems than that, but a partnership that blended a range of skills and once made sense may impede your opportunity to optimize the return from your assets. Partnerships can be a great way to own and manage real estate, but as time and markets change, the original use and deal structure may not continue to make sense. The partner you chose for his or her property management skills may not be the asset management partner you need under changed circumstances.

6. Net Lease Deals May be Your Answer. There's a growing asset class in real estate investing that involves buying net lease deals. There are many varieties of net leases, but most offer the investor the opportunity to buy a property and lease it back to a tenant. The tenant generally is responsible for the maintenance of the property and the payment of taxes and insurance. If the tenant has full operating expense responsibility, then the lease is termed a triple net lease. That means the tenant is responsible for the three main operating cost components of the property: maintenance, insurance, and real estate taxes. Other net leases may be termed double net, in which the tenant pays taxes and insurance, but the landlord maintains responsibility for components of the operating expenses like the walls and roof.

In a subset of net lease investments, the owner invests only in the land and has no ownership in the improvements. Such land net lease deals are the least complicated, so they often support lower cap rates. Many of the retail businesses you're familiar with occupy net lease properties. That includes many variants of so-called dollar stores, fast food restaurants, branch banks, medical facilities, daycare centers, and a wide range of others. Net lease deals frequently are higher dollar investments that require considerably less management. They sell at prices that are a function of the credit quality of the tenant, the term of the lease, the level of owner involvement, and the risk in property expenses. The better the credit of the tenant and the longer the term of the lease and the closer to triple net, the lower the cap rate and the higher the price for the property.

There Are Other Ways to Invest in Real Estate.

When is investing in real estate not like owning and operating a business? It's when you invest in a Real Estate Investment Trust (REIT). There are all kinds of REITs. Some invest in net lease deals, shopping malls, or retail properties, and others invest in housing, warehouses, and self-storage. There are even REITs that invest in data centers and records storage facilities. There are two basic kinds of REITs: equity REITs, which own the various kinds of real estate, and mortgage REITs (mREITs), which invest in debt secured by real estate. REITs are mostly products of the income tax code because they avoid corporate income tax on their earnings as long as they distribute at least 90 percent of their earnings to investors. And, yes, there are Dividend Champion REITs.

We don't currently invest in REITs, Dividend Champion or otherwise. We still own a significant amount of real estate in its own right and have avoided investing in real estate through public market opportunities like REITs. That may change as we continue to divest individual real estate investments and withdraw from operating the real estate business that such investments require. Maybe our aversion to REIT investments after all these years of investing in various aspects of real estate is more personal. Maybe it's as if a guy who's successfully operated restaurants all his life finds it a bit uncomfortable to invest in restaurant stocks.

There's a big advantage to REITs in that they're liquid.

There's a big advantage to REITs in that they're liquid. You can readily buy and sell your interest in a REIT. A big disadvantage of owning real estate itself is its illiquidity. To buy or sell, you usually need to hire a broker and go through a laborious and often expensive process to acquire and dispose of real estate. Then, of course, there's all the effort involved in managing real estate.

Investing in Dividend Champion REITs is generally much like investing in real estate but without all the time, energy, and risk of managing a real estate business. I've invested in the various aspects of real estate for fifty years. It's hard for me to think in terms of not doing that. But if REITs had been available back then, and if it were as easy to invest in real estate and its many aspects years ago as it is today, I would have saved a huge amount of time and effort by investing in the much more liquid DC REITs. I wouldn't have the stories to tell and wouldn't have worked with all the people, but just think of all the time and energy I'd have had. Times change. You should rethink any decision to get involved in hands-on real estate investing, though, as a rule, the leverage there beats the devil out of the leverage that's safe when you invest in REITs or stocks.

In my family, we might be in the midst of a generational change. It's hard for me not to respond when an old colleague calls with a real estate deal. What do I say? "My children want me to invest in Dividend Champion REITs"? It's hard for me not to call on that for sale sign. It's hard not to scroll through that annual list of tax certificate sales. But markets change, and time and capital have their limits.

John J. Smith
1074 Summit Avenue
Miami, Florida 68342
918.632.xxxx
johnjsmith12@internet.com

FINANCIAL STATEMENT
October 31, 2019

I. CASH	$135,000
II. STOCKS & BONDS	$5,098,853
III. REAL ESTATE	$1,535,000
IV. PARTNERSHIPS	$2,088,582
V. RETIREMENT	$891,000
VI. OTHER	$38,000
TOTAL ASSETS	$9,786,435
TOTAL LIABILITIES	$1,042,266
NET WORTH	$8,744,169

10.65%
%LIABILITIES/ASSETS

John J. Smith   3.31.19
JOHN J. SMITH   DATE

ASSETS

I. CASH			$135,000
A. PERSONAL	I-1	$95,000	
B. CERTIFICATES OF DEPOSIT	I-2	$40,000	
II. SECURITIES			$5,098,853
A. ABC BROKERAGE	II-1	$3,972,000	
B. DEF BROKERAGE	II-2	$1,126,853	
III. REAL ESTATE			$1,535,000
A. 106 OAK ST.	III-1	$385,000	
B. 1210 WALNUT ST.	III-2	$280,000	
C. 642 SYCAMORE AVE.	III-3	$495,000	
D. 342 8TH AVE	III-4	$375,000	

ASSETS

I. CASH					$135,000
A. PERSONAL	I-1	$95,000			
B. CERTIFICATES OF DEPOSIT	I-2	$40,000			

II. SECURITIES					$5,098,853
A. ABC BROKERAGE	II-1	$3,972,000			
B. DEF BROKERAGE	II-2	$1,126,853			

III. REAL ESTATE					$1,535,000
A. 106 OAK ST.	III-1	$385,000			
B. 1210 WALNUT ST.	III-2	$280,000			
C. 642 SYCAMORE AVE.	III-3	$495,000			
D. 342 8TH AVE	III-4	$375,000			

IV. PARTNERSHIPS					$2,088,582
	INTEREST	MKT VALUE	LOAN	NET	
A. DPM PARTNERS					
1. MORT NOTES IV A-1	50.00%	$320,000	$0	$160,000	
2. LAND IV A-2	50.00%	$150,000	$540,000	$75,000	
B. FAIRFAX PARTNERS IV B	40.00%	$1,700,000	$295,000	$464,000	
C. FAIRFAX PARTNERS 2 IV C	33.00%	$600,000	$550,000	$305,000	
D. MCLEAN OFFICE PARTNERS IV D	33.30%	$804,000	$1,130,000	$84,582	
E. DC WAREHOUSES IV E	40.00%	$2,300,000	$0	$468,000	
F. 3750 10TH ST NE IV F	50.00%	$750,000	$465,000	$375,000	
G. LOFTON CREEK PLAZA IV G	20.00%	$1,250,000		$157,000	
TOTALS		$7,874,000	$2,980,000	$2,088,582	

V. RETIREMENT					$891,000
A. STATE RETIREMENT SYSTEM	V-1	$250,000			
B. IRA	V-2	$641,000			

VI. OTHER					$38,000
A. CARS	VI-1	$33,000			
B. PERSONAL	VI-2	$5,000			

TOTAL ASSETS					**$9,786,435**

LIABILITIES

A. Mortgages			$665,949
1. 106 Oak St.	$109,990	A-1	
2. 1210 Walnut St	$109,990	A-2	
3. 642 Sycamore Ave.	$304,639	A-3	
4. 342 8th Ave	$141,330	A-4	
Total	**$665,949**		
B. Margin			$376,317
1. ABC Brokerage	$376,317		
TOTAL LIABILITIES			$1,042,266
NET WORTH			**$8,744,169**

NOTES

Cash
I-1 Personal checking account at First Federal of FL (4014319) and money market acct at FFF (1071786) ; City First NB Acct #7634572 and City First Money Market Acct #3968754
I-2 CD at City First #76532 maturing 3.17.2020

Securities
II-1/ Account #4659872 with ABC Brokerage held in living trust consisting mostly of dividend stocks.
II-2/ Account #598763 with DEF Brokerage held in living trust consisting mostly of dividend stocks.

Real Estate
III-1/ Cottage in downtown McLean, VA. Rented for $1,600/month on annual lease. Purchased 2/01 for $206,000
III-2/ Single family dwelling in St. Augustine FL. Managed by Karen Trent ERA Purchased 8/94 at foreclosure for $54,000. Renovated 2013 at $10,000. Rent is $2000/mo. On annual lease started 9.15
III-3/ Three bedroom, 2 bath home in St. Augustine FL. Purchased 9.01 for $259000 with $20,000 in improvements since.
III-4/ 2 BR, 2 BA Condo in St. Augustine FL rented for $1650/mo since 6.16. Purchased 2.10 for $175,000.

Partnerships
IV A-1/ Short term mortgages. Other 50% interest owned by Thomas and Marilyn Sullivan
IV A-2/ Value of five lots in MD suburbs of Washington, DC taken in foreclosure and currently for sale.
IV B/ 6,000 office building in Fairfax Virginia rented to three tenants. Purchased 12.03. Thomas and Marilyn Sullivan own 40%. Michael Brown owns 20%.
Mortgage with First Federal NB
IV C/ Property adjoining Fairfax Partners property. 3 BR 2 BA single family home. Bought for $225K in 2004 for $2,800/month. T & M Sullivan own 40%, M. Brown owns 20%.
Mortgage with Southern Bank.
IV D/ 3,000 sq. ft. rental office building in McLean VA. Sullivans own 1/3 and Brown owns 1/3.
Mortgage with First Federal NB
IV E/ Four warehouse units at 536 Avenue A NE, Washington DC in partnership with Sullivan (40%) and Brown (20%). Mortgage with Prince George NB
IV F/ Owns a day care center rented to operator. 50% owned by Sullivans.
IV G/ Estimated value of Lofton Creek property ($850K) plus note owed by First Right LLC ($400K). Mortgage is to Florida First.
Managing partner is Phil Graham (40%). Sullivans own 40%.

Retirement
V-1/ Retired Arkansas employee receiving an annuity of $34,881/year plus health insurance. Income subject to annual CPI adjustment. Amount shown approximate PV of annuity.
V-2/ Account number 3965432 with ABC Brokerage.

NOTES

Other

VI-1/ 2017 Lincoln Town Car. 2008 Toyota Tundra truck. No liens.
VI-2/ Value of personal property owned including furniture.

Mortgages

A-1/ Prime Mortgage #0599168473,
A-2/ Prime Mortgage #0599170420
A-3/ Citi Mortgage #1165809974
A-4/ First Federal #0018240200

Contacts:

1. Thomas and Marilyn Sullivan 202.365.xxxx
2. Mike Brown 202.362.xxxx
3. Phil Griffin 305.682.xxxx
4. First Federal National Bank, Bob Michaels 703.567.xxxx
5. Southern Bank, Tom Russo 703.310.xxxx
6. Prince George NB, Dan Snyder 301.563.xxxx
7. Florida First, Sally Wright 305.762.xxxx
8. Prime Mortgage, Louis Sikorski 305.843.000
9. Citi Mortgage, Karl Legore 305.912.xxx
10. ABC Brokerage, Kay Murphy 512.654.xxxx
11. DEF Brokerage, Mike McMahon 512.632.xxxx
12. Tax Accountant, Julian Sweet 904.362.xxxx
10. Karen Trent, ERA 305.254.xxxx
11. Property insurance and umbrella policy with Tom Angelini 904.361.xxxx
12. Attorney, Kevin O'Donnell 703.636.xxxx

13

BEYOND ESTATE PLANNING: SUCCESSION PLANNING

SOME YEARS AGO, WE HAD TWO ELDERLY FRIENDS die in close proximity to each other. They both had accumulated some wealth and had the requisite wills, revocable living trusts, durable power of attorney, and medical directives. They probably had gone to those estate planning seminars and dinners where you're encouraged to avoid probate by putting everything into a living trust. They had the standard package deal that most estate planning attorneys promote.

One friend divorced many years before his death and had two adult children by that marriage. He remarried and predeceased his second wife, also leaving a daughter with her young family from the second marriage. No one on the decedent's side of the family knew the extent of his estate. He was kind of your typical secretive guy when it came to his finances. On his death, it was learned that he'd left everything to his second wife. It was generally known that one of his children from the first marriage was in some financial distress, and his friends couldn't believe he hadn't made some special provisions for her. Needless to say, no one in his family—except his wife—knew anything about the details of his estate and his plan.

Circumstances were a bit different for our second elderly friend. His wife had died before him, and he was survived by three adult children. The youngest daughter had run into some financial problems in the years before her father's death, and her dad had helped her out financially. The decedent's will provided for equal distributions of his estate to the three children and appointed the oldest son as the executor. Simple enough. But the executor's first instinct was to withhold the father's earlier distributions from the younger daughter's share of the estate. He saw it as an early distribution and thought it was only fair to the other two siblings to reduce the younger daughter's share. But his other siblings objected, and it became a potentially contentious issue. Contention is not a good thing to have upon the death of a parent.

These are the kinds of problems and challenges common in families on the death of a parent who has significant assets. Estate planning tends to work like that no matter how well the decedent plans. A will typically provides for a division of property based on a formula. For example, if there are three children, then stocks and bonds are either sold or distributed in defined shares to the heirs. Less liquid assets such as real estate and businesses are to be sold and the proceeds distributed to the heirs as provided for in the will.

There were two major things that disturbed me about these two inheritance events. First, it seemed as if there were too many uncertainties, unknowns, and surprises. Most folks didn't know what the deceased owned and were uncertain as to the decedent's intents for distribution. Second, because the heirs didn't know much about the assets prior to death, there was a tendency to simply liquidate and distribute the proceeds. The tax code seemed to encourage liquidation. That's because if the value of the assets had appreciated, the assets could be sold or distributed without recognizing the gain for tax purposes. There still could be a tax due if the estate was large enough, but if not, there would be no taxable capital gain for each asset sale.

That seems to be the way many estates go. An executor administers the will and disposes of the decedent's assets as the will prescribes. Heirs often have very little advance knowledge of the particulars of the estate and have no prior knowledge of the decedent's plans for disposition.

> *. . . think about the way a corporation deals with its assets in anticipating and planning for future major transitions. A corporation has a duration beyond the lives of its leadership.*

Now, think about the way a corporation deals with its assets in anticipating and planning for future major transitions. A corporation has a duration beyond the lives of its leadership. A corporation presumes to go on forever, and to ensure the enterprise's continuing success, executives go to great lengths to design succession plans. Those are blueprints for making leadership decisions in advance of the retirement or death of the current executives. For example, shareholders are always inquiring about Warren Buffett's succession plan for Berkshire Hathaway. Buffett has most of his net worth in the stock of Berkshire, a vast conglomerate of diverse businesses. Buffett, no doubt, has a personal estate plan to direct the disposition of his individual assets, including his stock in Berkshire. But, as head of Berkshire, he has a duty to its stockholders to have a succession plan in place.

Considering these other estate planning events involving friends, it occurred to me that the interests of my heirs might be best served by selling nothing on my death. This may seem arrogant, but I've spent many years learning what I know about investing and asset management, and I think I now have it right. I've made every conceivable mistake, some of them multiple times. If a deceased version of myself could advise my heirs, he would likely say, "Just keep doing what I've been doing." I doubt they can do it better than I, at least initially. My principal heirs are my two children. They're highly educated, very smart people, and I've assembled a portfolio of assets that perform well. If kept intact, the assets will continue to grow nicely and provide a good living for the folks who manage those assets. I've accumulated and managed my assets to provide for the long-term well-being of my family, and I think my heirs should consider doing the same thing for their descendants.

The Process of Succession Planning

In the beginning, my children and I were like most folks. They had a rough idea of what I do but no specific knowledge of the details. And man, are there a lot of details! Since I have a tough time managing a wide array of assets, you can imagine the problems that could present to someone who stepped in suddenly and had to manage things. The turmoil would compound all the other problems and disruption associated with my passing. Realizing that, I started to lay out an approach to create a succession plan. I really had very little idea how such a plan would evolve or take shape at the time.

> *Since I have a tough time managing a wide array of assets, you can imagine the problems that could present to someone who stepped in suddenly and had to manage things.*

Some years ago, I talked to my family about what I saw as an inadequate, standard estate planning approach—based on how things went after the deaths of the friends I discussed above. I told them the same things I've written, and I also suggested that they consider managing our family assets in substantially the same way I had run them. To do that, they'd have to gain a working knowledge of everything we own, our partners, our lenders and bankers, our property managers, accountants, brokers, and insurers. I told them it would be a good idea for them to meet these folks and understand their roles now rather than at my funeral. After I'm gone, the business decisions will be theirs. If there's any hope for them to keep our asset management business intact with the best long-term returns, they have to become intimately knowledgeable about all the details of the business. That's how I came to think of the investments I had accumulated and grown over a lifetime. It's now an asset management business.

Following is an outline of the way things have evolved since those first discussions. I didn't specifically plan it this way, but over time, this is the process that developed:

1. At the end of every month, I sent my children a detailed Personal Financial Statement (PFS) that listed all assets and debts and the contact information for all the principals involved in all of our assets. This took a lot of effort at first, but after I'd compiled all the loan and account numbers, it's relatively little work to update each month. That way, on my death, the heirs have all the most current information necessary to pick up where I left off. See the PFS at the end of chapter 12 for an example.

2. I followed up the PFS with a monthly teleconference in which we discuss assets and their management and operation. We highlighted problems and opportunities and consider various approaches. These conversations have changed with time as my children have gained a more sophisticated understanding of various assets and their management. For example, some assets have been held in partnership for a long time, and the dynamic

among the partners has changed. It's essential that the children understand the interaction among the various partners.

3. Not too far into the process, I instituted a monthly stipend. The children spent time reviewing materials, participated in calls, and did some analytical work. I thought it appropriate to pay them a modest sum to cover their time and some costs. I eventually thought of them as a board of directors and felt they should at least get a meeting fee.

4. Also early in the process, the children took tours of our various real estate holdings. They met my partners, lenders, and property managers. Since they incurred some travel expenses, the monthly stipend seemed to make even more sense. They also met the brokers who handled our securities accounts. They even participated in discussions with the securities brokers, negotiating things like margin rates, training opportunities, and trading commissions. It was paramount that they learn everything is negotiable and how and when to negotiate.

5. I started to routinely copy the children on all important correspondence regarding our assets.

6. By this time, the children became increasingly assertive and were adding value. The fact is, the younger generation is just more astute at all things technological. I started to see a flow of suggestions on how better to structure and access data. One simple but hugely time-saving suggestion was that one of the children organized all the DCs on the *Yahoo Finance Watchlist* software, so we could promptly view them in the order of greatest daily declines. Up to that time, I'd used the *Wall Street Journal*'s page to identify the top one hundred decliners each day. Then I'd scroll down and, relying on my memory, identify the DCs on the list. Moving to *Yahoo* seems like an obvious move today, and it's saved me all kinds of time.

7. A year after I began implementing our succession planning process, I started to send my tax returns to the children. My return is very complex, but when they had the returns in hand, I could more easily discuss with my board of directors the role of taxes and the kinds of strategies we should use going forward. That proved particularly helpful in evaluating the 2018 tax code changes. By this time, I increasingly included the children in business decisions via our teleconferences, and I recognized they had morphed into the board of directors of our asset management business.

8. My board didn't agree with all my actions and investments, and over time they made that clear. Somewhere in the process, the board came to understand the real effort, time, and risk it took to develop and manage our real estate assets. They let me know they weren't big fans of one-off real estate investing, and they wanted to consider moving into less labor-intensive and time-consuming real estate DCs.

The sole stockholder (me) was reluctant to change, for reasons I perhaps couldn't fully explain to my board. I'd done real estate for so many years, it probably had become a habit. Many of my relationships were in the field, and it was hard for me to ignore a call from an old colleague about a prospective deal. How do you explain that your board discourages any hands-on real estate deals? You'd probably get a response like, "You have a board?" Then what do you say—"They're my children and grandchildren"? It's the truth, and it makes sense, but it sounds kind of lame. As of this writing, we're selling some of the lesser performing, labor-intensive real estate. My board is happy about that, as the capital goes mostly into DCs.

That said, I'm doing a small build-to-suit office building for one of our tenants in another property. What's the board's view? "Look, Dad, if you have to do it and it makes you happy, go ahead." I have a tough, but sometimes benevolent board. Maybe when they go to the opening of the new building, they'll get the feeling: lots of new jobs, happy customers, people expressing appreciation, the hands-on creation of wealth, and the extraordinary sense of accomplishment. I've learned in this process that the board's perspective may change with time and experience. But, then, mine might change too.

9. Prepare for surprises—almost all good ones, in my case. Here's one example from among many. I maintained one trading account with David, a financial advisor, and paid him the standard 1 percent financial advisory fee, which included all trading fees. I effectively trained the guy in my system of how to sell puts on DCs on dips and then DRIP the dividends. David managed the account similar to the way I manage my principal brokerage account.

Why have a separate account and pay the fee? Because early on I was never sure whether the children would develop the skills and interest to manage our securities. They might want to keep the portfolio intact but have David continue to manage it. A couple of things happened. First, I think David became a believer in the approach. The children also became believers and started to adopt the practices in their own investments, with some variations.

My son, Matt, for example, became an active options trader and refused to sell margin-backed puts. He insisted on having cash available to back his put sales. So, he'd sell a Hormel (HRL) put with a strike price of $40 only if he maintained $4,000 in cash. If he had a substantial gain on the put, he might buy it back and thereby release the $4,000 to be redeployed to other put sales. My daughter, Erin, also took great interest in stocks and options trading.

> *The day came when I was satisfied that*
> *both of my directors understood the system and the math.*

The day came when I was satisfied that both of my directors understood the system and the math. When I raised the prospect of bringing in the David portfolio, I asked both directors if they wanted to manage the account for the same fee I paid David. Matt was interested but wanted a share in the profits beyond the 1 percent. He thought that was warranted because he planned to be a more active and safer manager than I. Daughter Director Erin preferred my more structured approach and agreed to take on the task at the 1 percent fee, so she got the assignment. We undertook a training period, and she became proficient very quickly. I hadn't predicted that. Erin created another cash flow for herself, and we brought the work into the family and advanced the family's skills.

10. I think things will continue to evolve. Soon we will start discussions about transferring the balance of our securities to management by the directors and I will go on as less involved in securities trading but maybe more involved in something else. My children are engaging their children, and one day I expect the grandchildren to be involved in work related to the family's assets. In time, they too will receive compensation for their work.

It's all become so natural and part of our family life, I sometimes wonder what other parents discuss with their adult children.

The Family Office

I've also changed my thinking about what I do and my role. I now identify myself as running the Keogh Family Office. So, at those

Chamber of Commerce meetings when they go around the table, I now say, "I'm Pat Keogh, and I manage the Keogh Family Office." It's actually a business that manages a diverse portfolio of assets comprised mostly of securities and real estate. There are some other assets, such as mortgages and minor interests in operating businesses. I think of myself as the sole owner and CEO, subject to the direction and guidance of my board of directors—my children.

I have no way to know what will happen upon my death, but I think the business might continue as is. It's possible. Why split up a going concern that's working? The family assets will provide a secure and prosperous future for my children and their children if they continue to manage the assets as they are now. If my children continue to engage and train their heirs as I've involved them, then the assets will continue to grow into forever.

Another reason my business might continue in its current form is that my heirs—my directors—understand all the assets. There are no mysteries. They understand those assets held in partnerships. They know the partners and where I differ in views from those partners. There's little chance my directors would sell our partnership interests at a bargain price. They know the assets and the businesses and, perhaps most importantly, they understand the future opportunities for the assets. We're partners on assets in our nation's capital, and those properties are in the path of significant redevelopment, which means they're appreciating rapidly. Marketing or developing those properties is a complex and sophisticated undertaking but likely worth the effort to capture the added value in those assets. That's not something my children could have learned overnight, but as my directors, they've had years to gain a deep understanding of the future opportunities those partnership properties represent.

> *My directors also know all*
> *my creditors, property managers, and brokers.*

My directors also know all my creditors, property managers, and brokers. Having younger people involved gives lenders a certain sense of confidence in the security of their loans. They know that on my demise there will be someone to manage the business and pay the bills. Property managers know that an involved and informed younger generation will represent the ownership. My real estate and securities brokers also know my children and understand there will be no loss of momentum when I'm no longer involved. It all feels right, and with time, it just seems to get more comfortable.

Not a *King Lear* Deal

As you involve the next generation, you develop a different view of the business. With time, it becomes less *mine* and more *ours*, or even *theirs*. It makes sense to think that way. If things work the way they should, the next generations will spend more time and benefit more in the future from these assets than I will. In terms of present value, they'll likely derive the most value from the assets and the businesses they represent. Even though you don't survive, the business hopefully will, and in that way, maybe you can take it with you.

But this isn't a Shakespeare's *King Lear* transfer of property to the heirs during my life. King Lear ended as a tragedy for everyone. Mine is a transfer of knowledge and experience, so they gain the skills to continue to run the domain when I'm gone, and they take ownership under the terms of my estate plan. Lear transferred the valuables and believed his values went along with them. I think my approach is to pass on the valuables only after instilling the values that led to their accumulation.

Mine is a transfer of knowledge and experience, so they gain the skills to continue to run the domain when I'm gone, and they take ownership under the terms of my estate plan.

We're now at the point at which it's clear there may come a time in the not-too-distant future where we structure ownership of our assets differently. That is, we may transfer the various assets to a corporation or LLC. There could be some tax advantages to such a structure, but more importantly, a corporate or LLC structure could offer the opportunity to simply transfer stock in the entity rather than leave individual assets to heirs. We're in the early days of discussion on that topic—engaging our attorneys and tax advisers on the matter. If we hadn't done the things we have over the years, it wouldn't be practical to consider the possibility of such a structure.

I don't know what will happen when I'm gone, but as time passes and my succession plan takes root and evolves, I think the chances improve that my asset management business will stay intact, run by my children and grandchildren. That could mean the business continues to grow and provide them with a secure and prosperous future. I think a family succession plan is more a process than a destination. Our process seems well advanced, and I hope it will continue to evolve.

14

MOVE TO THE RICH
NEIGHBORHOOD

IN EVERY TOWN, THERE'S A REALLY RICH NEIGH-
borhood and a lot of no-so-rich neighborhoods. Everything
is much neater in the rich neighborhood. There's that old expression, "Birds of a feather flock together." Only rich folks live
in that rich neighborhood. The schools are better, the stores are
nicer, and everything seems to work better there. That's one of the
reasons governments and courts persist in trying to integrate those
places, particularly their schools. They even bus children from
poor families into the rich neighborhoods to expose the children to
better schools and the habits of rich people, in hopes that some of
that success and wealth will brush off. To make your family rich, it
will help to board the bus and transport yourself over to the rich
neighborhood.

But you're not rich yet, so how do you buy that big house in
the rich neighborhood? You don't. This is a new time, and all the
stuff that makes those folks rich is available to you without moving
from your couch. Sure, there are rich folks who inherit their wealth.
They barely do a lick of work, and they get more money than they
can count from Mom and Dad. There are lots of folks like that, but

you're not one of them. You also don't have to spend all that time with a shrink to help you work through all the problems people who inherit wealth often seem to have. Then there are those who win the lottery and buy the big house. You're not one of them either, so you don't have to fight off all those friends and relatives looking for a handout. You're going to make your family rich by earning it. Could it be simpler? Or better?

More important than the big fancy houses is what goes on in the rich neighborhood, and maybe just as important is what *doesn't* go on in the rich neighborhood. To make your family rich, you need to adopt the habits of successful people who earn their wealth and avoid the habits of unsuccessful people.

> *More important than the big fancy houses is what goes on in the rich neighborhood, and maybe just as important is what* doesn't *go on in the rich neighborhood.*

Read and Watch the Same Stuff as Your New Neighbors

As mentioned earlier, you are what you read and what you watch on TV. You're also what you wear and how you look and speak. These things have almost nothing to do with real estate and who your neighbors are. Earlier, we suggested publications you need to read. Every day, you should read the *Wall Street Journal*, and every week, you need to read *Barron's*. If they're new to you, it might take some time to learn the vocabulary in these publications. But you'll soon become familiar with the concepts and the lexicon. The process will be faster if you adopt our program and invest in DCs. You'll then be a business person who owns various businesses, and you'll need and want to stay informed about all the things that affect the economy and your businesses.

You should have CNBC on during the day and perhaps watch some of their business shows in the evening. It's most important to have CNBC on during the day when you're at home. You're learning a new language—or maybe a dialect of your mother tongue. These are your businesses, and you'll occasionally see the people who manage your businesses interviewed on the various CNBC shows. Those guys now work for you. You'll see securities analysts who specialize in your businesses give their views of the future of those businesses. They're there to help you evaluate all those managers who work for you.

Your smart phone should have the *Seeking Alpha, Yahoo Finance Watchlist*, and *CNBC* apps. *Seeking Alpha* is particularly important. That's where you get to talk over the fence with your neighbors in your rich neighborhood about the businesses you own or are considering for investment. You drop in on all the businesses you own in your neighborhood, whether that's McDonald's, Walgreens, or Walmart. That's what the guys in the rich neighborhood do. They check up on the businesses they own or manage. The businesses you own are all over town. Go visit them. Buy from them. Recommend them to your friends. That's what business owners do.

Education is Key

The educational level of the folks in the rich neighborhood is always higher than folks elsewhere. Are they rich because they're educated, or are they educated because they're rich? Sure, there are guys with limited educations who are very wealthy, but most wealthy folks are educated. Don't fight it. Never before in history has quality education been so readily available to everyone. You don't even have to leave your home to go to that great school in the rich neighborhood. It's all available online. If you can go off to college, whether four-year or a community college, you should. Period. Higher education makes you a better person and a better citizen. Don't buy into the nonsense that college is not for everyone. It is.

> *…if you think you can't go to college for whatever reason or don't want to go to college, there's no excuse to not always be taking classes in something.*

But if you think you can't go to college for whatever reason or don't want to go to college, there's no excuse to not always be taking classes in something. It's all available online, and education is of high value to rich people. You need to embrace that value and pass it on to your successors. It needs to be part of your succession plan. Remember, the valuables shouldn't transfer until the values transfer.

Maybe even more important than the things you need to do in the rich neighborhood are the things rich people don't do.

No Self-Graffiti

It's important to inoculate yourself against diseases that will either prevent you from becoming rich or make it more difficult. Let's start with personal graffiti. There's a particularly virulent disease attacking our young people that prevents them from being successful and rich. That's what tattoos are, and most people in the rich neighborhood don't have tattoos.

You've heard all the nonsense about tattoos being a form of self-expression or body art. I even read about a guy who said the permanence of tattoos is an important part of their attraction in a world that seems to be spiraling out of control. Perhaps he should stop drinking or smoking the stuff that has him spinning. He said a tattoo is something tangible, something you can't lose that will be with you for life. So is syphilis, but you don't voluntarily induce the disease.

You might like some graffiti. You may think you saw some cool graffiti on a truck or a bridge or a subway car. You dug the colors and the bold, original images. They may even have written articles about your favorite graffiti artist, El Supremo, in the Sunday art section of the New York Times. Let's suppose El Supremo owns his own home. I know that's a stretch, but let's just suppose this guy owns a home. Could you possibly imagine his being so stupid as to graffiti his own home? Of course not. It would destroy the value of his property. Even El Supremo gets that. So why would you graffiti your own body? Think about it. You want to buy a new home and you drive into the neighborhood past a number of graffiti-covered buildings. Does that make a positive first impression? Of course not! So, what kind of impression do you think you make when you have tattoos?

You're not going to be Angelina Jolie. I'm sorry to be the one to break that news. Sure, she has tattoos, and she's rich. She's the exception. There's an exception to every rule. Let someone else be the exception. All you have to do is watch one of those TV shows about prison life. It's apparently common for prisoners to form into gangs behind bars. The blacks have their gangs, as do Latinos, and whites have various Arian brotherhoods. They all have tattoos. These guys are in prison because they're losers. They all may have stories about being victims of something or other, but they're losers, and they all have tattoos. Losers don't get rich.

I worked with a young man in a restaurant I owned. He was a nice guy who seemed to be wired right, but he and his wife had a number of tattoos. Their wedding rings were even tattooed on their ring fingers. They have two young daughters, so when I told him what I thought about tattoos, I asked how he was going to handle the inevitable questions from his daughters as they grew up. He responded that he wouldn't allow them to get tattoos until they were eighteen, and after that the decision would be theirs. Nice, neat answer, but it told me he didn't think a tattoo was a good idea for his daughters. When they were eighteen, the decision was no longer his. I responded, "What, they're not your daughters after they turn eighteen? If they're still your daughters, and you're still their father, and you know it's a bad idea, then what does it matter how old they are? Just tell them you made a mistake, and tattoos aren't a good idea for them or anyone else unless they're Maori warriors."

Most people will be parents someday. If you have self-graffiti, how do you explain that to your son or daughter? "I only have one, and it's a beautiful butterfly or bird." Once you have one and communicate to your child that self-graffiti is okay, how do you tell your child that fourteen tattoos are not okay? Where is the limit to self-graffiti? Check out those guys in the prison yards. Their entire bodies are covered, and every one of those guys started with one.

Not long ago, I was in one of those overnight delivery stores in Florida. It was a warm day but cold in the store. A young man, let's call him Mark, assisted me. He wore a small badge that identified him as a trainee. His long-sleeve shirt was unbuttoned at the cuff, and I could see he had tattoos on both arms above the wrists. He looked as if he was his late twenties and had a very helpful and outgoing personality. I asked how long he'd worked there. He said it had only been a couple of months. We talked about his prior employment, and Mark was very forthcoming with the fact that he was married and had two young daughters.

When I asked about the tattoos, he told me his employer had initially rejected his job application. Mark made further inquiries and found that the company's personnel manual allowed tattoos as long as they were concealed. When he brought that to the company's attention, he said they reluctantly hired him on the condition he keep the tattoos covered. That explained the long-sleeved shirt and also the excess air conditioning. Mark and I hit it off pretty well, so I pressed forward on my mission.

"So, what are you going to tell your daughters about tattoos?" I asked.

"First off," Mark replied, "we don't call them tattoos around my house. We call them job killers."

It was clear that Mark had learned the lesson. When I asked, "Why don't you get them removed?"—a question I frequently ask of graffitied young people—I got the standard response: "Do you have any idea how much that costs and how painful removal is?"

I built a restaurant some years ago. Actually, I converted an old gas station to a restaurant. There were lots of complications and costs associated with that. In the process, I befriended two laborers; let's call them Butch and Tommy. Both were about twenty. Both were hard-working, nice guys. One day, I drove up in my old battered Chevy S10 truck. I have a number of properties that need work, so a truck made sense, and I'd bought the S10 at a government auction. It was old but functional. I could schlep stuff to a job site and get solid gas mileage. It had low miles and low operating expenses. The insurance cost was minimal, and I didn't need collision insurance.

Butch, Tommy, and I became friends. One day when I arrived at the site, Tommy approached me and said, "You know, Pat, a guy like you needs a newer, bigger truck." When I asked why, he simply repeated, "A guy like you just needs a bigger, newer truck," as though repetition would convince me of the error of my ways. I said, "Look, Tommy, this truck is paid for. It does the job I need it to do, and it requires a minimum insurance cost." Tommy persisted that my old S10 Chevy didn't match my image as a restaurant developer.

We were in the parking lot outside the soon-to-be restaurant. I noticed Tommy had a tattoo on his left arm, a monkey smoking what I thought was a cigarette. When I inquired about the tattoo, Tommy responded that it was Sam, an orangutan at a local zoo where his father managed the monkey or simian house. It turns out that his dad was smoking a marijuana cigarette with a buddy when Sam observed the goings-on. When Tommy's dad laid the joint down, Sam picked it up and took a toke. Tommy's dad went home and told the story to his family, and it impressed Tommy enough to go out and self-graffiti the event. How's that for quality parenting?

The story gets better from here, or worse, depending on your perspective. On Tommy's right arm was an ugly scar. Fascinated by the Sam story, I asked, "What's that all about?" Tommy declined to answer. As we shared life experiences in that parking lot, I persisted. Butch interjected, "That's about Lisa." I asked, "Who's Lisa?" to Tommy's discomfort. Butch told me, "That's Tommy's ex, and when she dumped Tommy, he cut out her tattoo." Apparently, Tommy had a *Tommy loves Lisa* tattoo on his right arm, and when Lisa ended the relationship, Tommy took a knife to his arm and cut out the tattoo. Can you feel that pain? Did I mention how permanent tattoos are and how expensive they are to remove?

So, here was a young man who presumed to give me lifestyle and career counseling on my choice of vehicle, but he'd engaged in some of the most senseless behavior imaginable when it comes to self-graffiti. How crazy is that?

Tattoos are the single worst thing a young person can do to sabotage his or her success. They also act as magnets to attract other folks with tattoos. If you doubt that, remember those prison photographs you've seen. Remember that old adage, "Birds of a feather flock together." All those graffitied guys in the prison yard are jailbirds. You think the fact they're all graffitied is a coincidence?

Sure, there are exceptions. About 23 percent of all Americans have tattoos. Shockingly, some 40 percent of those between eighteen and twenty-nine are self-graffitied. We always hear that the new generation of Americans won't be as prosperous as the last. Maybe self-graffiti has something to do with that. A Pew Research Center survey found that 76 percent of those surveyed believe that tattoos hurt an applicant's chances of being hired. Forty-two percent of respondents feel that tattoos are always inappropriate at work.

> *A Pew Research Center survey found that 76 percent of those surveyed believe that tattoos hurt an applicant's chances of being hired.*

Tattoos are negative for your job and earning prospects. Here, though, is the most shocking data. Only 4 percent of those with tattoos report having faced actual discrimination. What that tells me is that graffitied people aren't being told that the tattoos are hurting them. I guess that's a job left to me.

There's a gender thing going on too. Women are more than twice as likely to have tattoos, and single and divorced people are much more likely to have tattoos than those who are married.

You could become the next Angelina Jolie or an NBA or NFL star. If that's your plan, then lots of luck, and we'll see you on the big screen. Self-graffiti doesn't make you a better actor, nor does it do anything to improve your jump shot, so why take the chance that you'll get rich despite the graffiti?

Finally, it's not just tattoos that adversely affect your future. The Pew Research Center survey found that body piercings have the same effect. Does anyone really think that a ring in his or her nose looks appealing to anyone, with the possible exception of someone else with a nose ring?

We need a come-to-Jesus moment here. My father and mother were immigrants. My father worked in ship yards before he immigrated to the US. Somewhere along the way, he acquired an anchor tattoo on his right wrist. He never talked about it, but we children sensed he was embarrassed about the tattoo. We understood neither to ask him about it nor—under any circumstances—to repeat his mistake. So, people make mistakes. If you have the funds, get the mistakes removed. If funds aren't available, don't repeat the mistake, and cover the mistakes you've made. Then seek redemption by taking every opportunity to counsel others, particularly younger people, not to make the same mistake.

Speech as Verbal Graffiti

In your new neighborhood, people speak correctly. You need to make sure you do too. When a young person interviews for a job, applies to a school, or meets with a loan officer, he or she is probably dealing with someone like me. I'm older, a bit conservative, and I want to work with someone who has good habits—someone I can count on to be intelligent, get the job done, meet obligations, and represent our business in a professional manner. I want to deal with someone who shows good judgment. I'm not your friend, and I really don't need to understand that deep down you're a good person. Some old expressions make compelling sense, like, "You never get a second chance to make a first impression." It's important in business and personal matters to make good first impressions by looking and sounding like a responsible person. Other adages that convey a different message just don't make sense. For example, "You can't tell a book by its cover." No one in a position of responsibility really believes that. Whether they admit it or not, most people who make decisions about things like employment, schools, and lending have negative views of people with poor communication skills. It's just the way it is; deal with it. What's important is that the people who make decisions in matters like jobs, education, and lending control your path to wealth.

> *Your speech tells as much about you as tattoos.*

Your speech tells as much about you as tattoos. That's why I think of poor language skills as verbal graffiti. Just listen to those guys in the prison yard—the same guys with the tattoos. They routinely use foul language, double negatives, and the incorrect tense, not to mention poor sentence structure. If you want to compete to be the "baddest" guy in the yard, it helps to say things like, "That m——f—— be in my face, and there ain't no way he be gettin' away with that s—!" Now, anyone who hears that will readily understand the message: the speaker has been offended by a colleague and is planning some, as yet uncertain, unpleasant retribution. We understand the message, but the speaker sounds like a moron—albeit, presumably a dangerous fellow with a surfeit of testosterone, but a moron, nonetheless. His statement fulfills the basic purpose of speech, which is communication, but it says much more about the speaker, and none of it's good, unless you're the promoter for the reality show *Really Bad Ass Prison Morons*.

To speak correctly, you should also avoid the use of filler words. Filler words are those words and expressions that add no meaning to your communication other than to communicate your lack of language proficiency. These are the "like," "you know," "know what I'm saying?" and "right" that are sprinkled throughout conversation but add no value or meaning to what's being said. There are few things more uncomfortable that listening to a young person's speech with "like" used in virtually every sentence. Here's how it sounds: "I was, like, having dinner with John when he, like, broke the news to me that he was, like, moving to New York, you know?" That excerpt is from a conversation among three young women in nearby seats on a recent flight. One of her companions responded, "That's, like, bad news. Did John, like, give you a reason?" The conversation continued that way and had the same effect on me as hearing chalk screech across a blackboard. It made me think the young women probably didn't share an IQ of one hundred among the three of them.

But there can be a life lesson in your poor speech. Let's say you have a "like" habit. You probably don't know how you contracted that disorder; it just gradually worked its way into your speech. Promise yourself to stop using "like" inappropriately. I've had younger members of my family commit to do that, and they found it remarkably difficult to break the habit. It's easy to develop a bad habit but enormously difficult to break one.

These are just some of the things that characterize folks in the rich neighborhoods. You don't have to move there to adopt the same characteristics.

15

THE GUIDING PRINCIPLES AT A GLANCE

HERE'S A SUMMARY OF THE GUIDING PRINCIPLES in this book and the *Make Your Family Rich* system.

1. Adopt the goal to make your family rich.
2. Commit to save first, and spend only what's left over.
3. Open a brokerage account now.
4. Invest only in Dividend Champions (DC) unless you have a special expertise and interest, but then only invest in moderation.
5. Never buy a DC directly if you can sell a put instead. Always sell a put on a day when a particular DC drops a lot and with a strike price lower than the current price. The exception is if you do not have enough cash to cover the put. Then go ahead and buy one or a few shares.
6. Start thinking of your investments as having and managing a second, part-time job, which is to run your asset management business. Visit, patronize, and recommend your businesses to others.

7. If you have to scratch an itch and buy a stock other than a DC, do it, but only in moderation.

8. If you invest in real estate, understand it's a complex, time-consuming business. It's probably better for you to invest in REIT DCs.

9. Invest in a college education. Although you can make your family rich without a college degree, it will be tougher. You'll likely be a better person, parent, and citizen with a college degree.

10. After you've bought a DC, never sell unless it fails to increase its dividend, and then sell immediately.

11. Engage your family in your asset management business and pay them if they get involved and are productive.

12. Take all your dividends from DCs in Dividend Reinvestment Plans (DRIPs).

13. Move to the (virtual) rich neighborhood.

14. Maintain a close relationship with your securities broker. Negotiate everything.

15. Forget the idea of retirement. Your lifetime job will be to manage your family's asset management business.

EPILOGUE

NOW YOU'VE READ THE BOOK, AND MAYBE YOU buy the approach; it makes good sense to you. My advice to you is, don't believe a word of it. None. Maybe the best advice I ever got was from my eighth-grade teacher, Brother James. He said, "Believe nothing of what you hear and read, and maybe half of what you think you see." No skeptic, the good Brother; just very realistic.

At my age, I can reflect on all the settled science I've heard, the truths that have since been refuted. Eggs were bad for you, and now they're not. Margarine was invented as a substitute for butter because butter wasn't good for you, and now margarine is bad for you. Women were told mammograms were good for them, and then science found mammograms had no positive effect on breast cancer survival rates. Global leaders believe climate change is man-made and devote fortunes to carbon reduction, but other data calls global warming into question. Eighty-five percent of all women wear the wrong size bra. Live long enough, and you'll hear most things that are settled and sure called into question. Brother James knew that.

I'm sure you've heard of other systems and approaches to investing, and the proponents have been confident and convincing. You came away believing they made sense, and maybe you tried those systems, and they didn't work so well. I've done that too.

It might help to think of our approach like the process for buying a car. You like a particular make and model, so you read the reviews, go to the dealership, and get the brochure. The brochure says the object of your affection is the best at everything an auto does. That's what new car brochures do; they sell you just like I've tried to do in this book. Then you test drive the car. On your next trip, you rent that car and talk with the car rental folks about their experience with the car. Not everyone is this thorough, but it's a good model for decision making.

Don't believe a word of our story, but what do you have to lose by taking it out for a spin? Open the brokerage account. It doesn't cost anything. You'll probably need one eventually, no matter what system you employ. Set up your *Yahoo Finance Watchlist* that details all the DCs from Justin Law's spreadsheet. That doesn't cost anything. Keep an eye on the daily dips, and maybe pick one or two and sell a put. If it hits and you buy the stock, be thankful that you bought the stock for less than you would have if you'd invested in the stock directly. Then live with it, DRIP it and maybe buy the company's products, and let it be your company. If the put expires without executing, then enjoy the premium and think about doing it again.

It's kind of like fostering a dog.

It's kind of like fostering a dog. The dog moves in, and you take care of him and hope someone will come along and adopt him. But you start to like the guy, and when a really neat family offers to make a great home for the dog, you're delighted to see him off but kind of sad too. It could have been your dog or your company and now it's gone, but you have the memory of the relationship or the premium to console you. It's all good. See if you feel that way. If you do, then go foster another mutt, and sell another put, and keep doing that.

Over time, expose your children or other family members to the experience and opportunity. Sure, it's about money and making your family rich, but it's also a lifestyle. It's what you all do together. It could be about the family farm or the family restaurant, but for your family it's about all the American businesses you own and the process you used to acquire them. Look at all those cars at McDonald's; we own that. Don't forget to pick up the prescription at Walgreens; we own that. Look, there's a Sysco delivery truck; we own that. Let's stop for a Coke; we own that. We need gas, and there's an Exxon station; we own that. It will become a bond between you and your children, just as if you'd taught them animal husbandry or how to prepare Grandma's perfect sauce. With some luck, they might go off to an A&M university or culinary school to take the farm learning or cooking skills you gave them to another level. With proper education, each generation will do it all better than the last, whether it involves farming or stock investing.

You'll rarely hit the home run. The next Facebook or Microsoft isn't ever going to be one of your targets. The only exception, of course, is if you feel that itch that needs to be scratched. But there likely will never be a "here today and gone tomorrow" stock either. Our system is more the Steady Eddie form of getting rich—slow, sure, confident wealth growth through the market's business cycles of ups and downs. And every year, you get a raise, so the downside is a bit less of a risk.

If you're lucky, the market will tank, and the value of your businesses will go down—maybe not as much as the market, but it will go down. However, your income will still go up. While others are keeping score on value, you keep score on income, knowing the value will eventually recover and then some. You can afford to wait, because you're investing for your family, forever.

Listen to Brother James from all those years ago: "Believe nothing of what you hear or read." I hope he would add today, "But take this book and its system out for a spin."

ACKNOWLEDGMENTS

T
HERE ARE SOME PEOPLE WE'D LIKE TO THANK.
First, Ken Biggs and all the folks at the Austin Chapter of
the American Association of Individual Investors. Ken runs
the Special Interest Group (SIG) in Austin, Texas, and he arranged
for me to make a presentation at the SIG, focused on my family's
investment approach and succession plan. My daughter Erin and
her son, Victor, attended a subsequent meeting to answer members'
questions about their perspective. Those meetings sparked a surpris-
ing amount of interest, and I received a number of calls afterward.
That led to the idea that more fully documenting our system might
be of interest to others. That was the origin of this book.

Harvey Lewis is a retired firefighter and Florida public pension fund trustee who now serves on the Gainesville, Florida Police
and Firefighters Pension Plan. Harvey previously served as a trustee with the Fort Lauderdale Police and Firefighters Pension Board.
When Pat took a position as a director of a Florida municipal Police
and Firefighters Pension Board, Harvey offered freely of his time
and advice to mentor Pat through all pension investment matters.
Harvey is a smart, experienced, common-sense financial guy who
reviewed an early draft of this book.

David A. Love is a broker with Davenport & Company LLC (Suffolk, Virginia), who, together with his long-time sidekick Christy Rose, expertly and graciously managed Pat's backup account—the account Pat maintained in case the next generation showed little aptitude or interest in managing the system. Over many years, David and Christy gave freely of their time to help manage the system outlined in this book. They were particularly understanding when the next generation showed proficiency, and Pat moved his backup account to Erin to manage. David also commented on a draft of this book. You just can't go wrong working with David and Christy.

Kay Russell is currently with the Austin, Texas office of TD Ameritrade. Pat has worked for years with TD Ameritrade and its predecessor organization. Kay has been generous with her time and insight to access the full range of TD Ameritrade's very talented staff. TD has great software, particularly for trading options, and wonderful, smart people in the back office to help clients work with their software. Kay has been a patient participant and advocate in our regular efforts to negotiate fees and rates. You can't go wrong working with Kay and TD Ameritrade.

Tom and Marilyn Sherman have been our long-term partners in all things real estate. They've been smart, hard-working colleagues to create much of the wealth that gave us the opportunity to expand into securities investing many years ago. They also starred in many of the tragic comedies outlined in the book's real estate chapter. Sometimes it was tough, but we always made money and continue to do so.

Fran Clark is Patrick's wife and partner. Her love, constant support, and patience helped make the time and atmosphere available to get this book finished.

ABOUT THE AUTHOR

Patrick J. Keogh manages the family office that handles the assets of the Keogh family. The office holds securities of the kind recommended in this book. The office also manages a portfolio of real estate assets, but over time, that's migrating from real estate to dividend champions. He still does an occasional development deal. Old habits are tough to break.

Pat was born, raised, and educated in the Bronx. He started work at age fourteen, selling hot dogs and peanuts for Harry M. Stevens Inc. at Yankee Stadium and other area sports venues. His professional career was focused as a financial and real estate development executive with the US General Services Administration. He left government service in 1994 and went into private practice, specializing in public-private partnerships for development projects. Pat is a certified pension trustee and was chairman of the board of a Florida municipal pension plan. He is a graduate of Manhattan College in the Bronx and the Georgetown University Law Center night school in Washington, D.C. Pat is a member of the Virginia Bar and the American Association of Individual Investors.

www.ingramcontent.com/pod-product-compliance
Lightning Source LLC
Chambersburg PA
CBHW060307220326
41598CB00027B/4260